You Gotta™

Get In The Game

Playing to Win in Business, Sales and Life

Billy Cox

CornerStone
Leadership Institute

www.**CornerStoneLeadership**.com

You Gotta
Get In The Game

Printed in the United States of America
ISBN: 0-9746403-3-6

Credits

Contributing Editor	Juli Baldwin, The Baldwin Group, Dallas, TX
Design, art direction, and production	Melissa Monogue, Back Porch Creative, Plano, TX
Cover	Bill Buck, GCG Advertising, Ft. Worth, TX

Presented to:

_____

By:

_____

Date:

_____

HOW TO GET THE MOST FROM THIS BOOK

When I was 20 years old, I knew I would write a book. Eight years later I got started, and now, another eight years later, it's finished. If you really want to know what's in it, *you gotta* **read it!**

As you read, keep a highlighter and some removable sticky "flags" nearby. Highlight key ideas and then flag those pages for easy future reference. I especially recommend marking the passages that discuss action steps you want to take. After all, knowledge without action is meaningless. Flagging action steps encourages you to follow through.

Remember, too, that leaders share what they learn. While you read, think about others who might benefit from this information. Then, share your learning with them.

So enjoy the book, make the most of it, share it with others and *Get in the Game*!

Acknowledgements

As with anything of significance, the completion of this book involved a great team.

I want to start by thanking Lisa O'Dell, Larry Liner and Bill Osborn – without your input, help, ideas and research, this book would not be the same. To Nancy Angelo, thank you for your patience, understanding and the time you graciously gave to help with this project; I couldn't have done it without you. I wish to thank Bryan Dodge for your review of this book, the encouragement you've given me, and for introducing me to Cornerstone Leadership; you truly helped make this dream a reality. To my friend and neighbor Kent Barry, I owe you a debt of gratitude for the time and effort you volunteered and the input you've given to make this book possible.

Special thanks to David Cottrell and Cornerstone Publishing for going absolutely nuts dealing with me on this project. I am grateful to Melissa Monogue for your ideas on the cover and interior design and to Scott Turner and Bill Buck for sharing your time and resources for the cover. To Juli Baldwin, thank you for the extra work you've given this project – the time you've taken to go back and forth with me, the editing, and the many finishing touches you've added.

A very special thank you to Ray and Toni Jones and the Jones family for giving me the opportunity to run your company. My heartfelt thanks go to our entire leadership team: Bill and Lara Kellett, Gene and Daune Melvin, Jack and Arlene Mohler, Craig and Julie Schwienebart, Gene and Carolyn Shelton, Larry and Patty Smith, Dale Archer, Dale and Deborah Ruschy, Justin and Sharon Wolbers, Jeff and Susan Lamb, and Marco and Deborah Gonzalez. Without your support, I never could have taken over the presidency and achieved the things we've accomplished together.

To A.V. and Wanda Holden, thank you for always being fair and for being like second parents to Susan and me. Thanks also to Mickey Frye for teaching us that every day can be a "payday" and a holiday. My appreciation to Kim Havens for being organized enough for all of us. And to Chris and Becky Roberts, my deepest gratitude for your tremendous support over the years and for everything you have contributed to our lives and our business. Deserving of special attention are James and Cindy Wilkerson for always being there and for stepping up and helping out when we needed you the most. Mostly, my thanks go to every single member of our team for making our mission possible.

I also wish to thank the many people who have influenced my life. To Gene Shelton, thank you for recruiting me into sales, and to Doug Shelton, thank you for being my first sales trainer. To Zig Ziglar, you have been an inspiration to me since I was just a kid; I don't think you have a book I haven't read or an audio I haven't listened to. Thanks also to Tony Robbins for absolutely inspiring me to take charge and believe that anything is possible using the techniques in your Personal Power program. I am grateful to John Maxwell and Jim Rohn for your great leadership training and to Ed Foreman for teaching us all that life is terrific. To Jim Madrid, many thanks for your help and insight regarding the Reticular Activating System and the power of visualization. Thanks also to

Tony Jeary for helping me understand that life really is "a series of presentations."

I especially want to thank my friend and mentor Charlie "Tremendous" Jones. You are one of the greatest men I have ever met.

My appreciation goes to the Fellowship Church and Pastor Ed Young, Jr. for your cutting-edge, inspiring messages which have undoubtedly impacted my life. And a very special thanks to Joel Osteen for the positive motivational messages you give each Sunday that have taught me a lot.

Finally, I want to give special thanks to my family. To my mother, Mary Updegrove, and father, Eugene Cox, without your guidance in my life there is no telling where I might be. Thanks also to my sisters Shirley, Deborah, Sherry and Candy. To my grandmother, Nelly Cox, I hope I am still in the game, like you are, when I am 84.

To my children – Blake, Chase, Connor and Destany – you are the greatest kids in the world. Life has something special in store for each of you. Remember that the sky is the limit. To my daughter Skylar, you are an angel. God chose you to go to Heaven, and I know we will see you again someday.

And to my wife, Susan, thank you for being patient and allowing me to burn the midnight oil to complete this book. But most of all, thank you for just being who you are; for sharing your life, love and dreams with me; and for the support you've always given me even when it wasn't deserved. I would never be the person I am today without your love and support.

Table of Contents

Introduction

In the game of life, there are no time outs, no overtimes. You only get one chance to play the game. The question *you gotta* ask yourself is, "At what level do I want to play – do I want to wait on the sidelines of life or do I want to win?"

If you want to win, ***you gotta get in the game***!

Although I've never made a dime as a professional athlete, I have discovered there are many similarities between success in sports and success in sales, business and life in general. In sports, it's not uncommon for two athletes with the same talents, skills and abilities to perform at dramatically different levels. One might be an average player while the other is a superstar.

The same is true outside of sports. Oftentimes someone will sell twice as much or make many times the income of others who have the same basic talents and skills. They may also live happier, more successful and productive lives. In fact, the superstars in business and in life frequently have less education and experience than the average performers, and yet they achieve extraordinary levels of success. Why?

Because they have a game plan – a strategy for winning the game – and a coach to help them implement it. If you want to win, this book will be your game plan, and I will be your coach. I'll provide you with a strategy for winning and teach you the rules of the game.

Early in my life, I was fortunate enough to study and learn the concepts, traits, habits and techniques that distinguish high performers from those who only get average results. Through my studies and personal experiences, I discovered a concept I call "the winning edge." The basic idea is that small improvements in key areas of your business and your life can lead to enormous differences in results. To put it another way, only small differences separate the superstars from the average performers.

Many people play the game but never win. People fail because they don't do the little things that will give them the edge it takes to win. As a result, they're playing to lose without even realizing it.

This book was written to show you how to get the winning edge so you can compete at the highest level. It's easy to read and straight to the point. The strategies and techniques are tried and true – they work. They have worked in my life, and I have seen them work time and time again in the lives of many others.

To get the full effect of this book, you must first understand that when I started out in sales, I was very young, inexperienced and flat broke. Over a period of 15 years, I worked my way to the top of every sales and management level and eventually became President and Chief Operating Officer of the same company I started with.

Throughout this journey, I made many mistakes but learned many lessons, experienced many triumphs but faced many adversities. I'm living proof that your past doesn't have to dictate your future. High achievers in all walks of life have ups and downs, victories and setbacks. Learning how others have turned their setbacks into comebacks can give you the inspiration and the determination to follow through and get the winning edge.

As you read, you'll notice how much I use the phrase *you gotta*. Though it may not be proper grammar, it is a powerful phrase for emphasizing important techniques and steps for success. *You gotta* means *you absolutely must*. All of us have a list of things we should do: we should save more money; we should get in shape; we should take a vacation; we should make those extra sales calls. *You gotta* turn your shoulds, coulds, woulds, mights and maybes into absolute musts if you want to achieve lasting success.

So, when you come across the *you gottas*, pay special attention and read very carefully. They identify the steps that are crucial to getting and keeping the winning edge. When you learn and apply all the *you gottas*, you will experience a massive increase in all areas of your business and life.

I believe that inside of you there is a champion. You have the potential to play your game at any level you choose. You can sit on the sidelines and watch others win, or you can jump in and play with strength, purpose, passion and power. You can be a spectator, or you can be a superstar.

My hope is that by reading this book, you will decide to set some goals and stretch yourself. I hope you're willing to discipline yourself. I hope you want to compete and that you will develop a burning desire to win. I hope you will make the decision to **Get in the Game**.

Billy Cox

1 You Gotta Get Off the Bench

I've never seen anyone make a shot **from the bench** or catch a touchdown from the sideline. I've never seen a top producer sit around waiting for someone to call and buy his or her products or services. In order to have any chance at winning, *you gotta* get off the bench and get into the game!

You can't sit on the bench and be a superstar. There are plenty of benchwarmers. *You gotta* want to be in the game! *You gotta* want it with an unstoppable, driving desire!

Star athletes can't "stand" to sit. It doesn't matter if the team is 20 points ahead or 20 points behind; they want to be part of the action. That's why they're superstars. A superstar can't wait for the next play, and a super salesperson can't wait to give the next presentation or close the next sale. True superstars take the initiative to get in the game; they make things happen.

> *"It is in your moments of decision that your destiny is shaped."*
>
> – Anthony Robbins

You Gotta Make a Decision

If you want to get off the bench, the first thing *you gotta* do is make a decision. A decision is a definite, conscious choice to do something. People make decisions every day, but make most of them without much thought or commitment behind them.

Through my experiences, I've discovered that the top performers in any profession always make a conscious, committed decision to be the best. They leave themselves no "outs." They say to themselves, "No matter what, I'm going to do it. That's it. Period."

Making a conscious decision to do something is one of the defining differences between people who achieve great results and those who achieve mediocre results. They both have more or less the same abilities and opportunities – it comes down to who is willing to make a decision and take action.

The first major turning point in my career involved a decision. When I started in sales, I was 17, fresh out of high school and flat broke. So I decided I would try sales part-time to make a little extra money. But I wasn't committed; I wasn't in the game. I looked at sales only as a way to make money, and as a result, my career was like a roller coaster – there were months I rose to the top and months I plunged to the bottom.

I remember one month specifically. It was the worst month of my sales career. I made one sale for a $100 commission, but it cost me $500 in expenses to make that sale! By the end of the month, I was discouraged and had lost all my confidence. I was sick and tired of the situation I had created and seemed trapped in. I was tired of my income – or rather, lack of income – tired of borrowing money from my parents, tired of the car I drove, and tired of my lackadaisical efforts and work habits.

I started to think I wasn't cut out for sales and began looking for a different job. I soon realized that in any job, I would still have to show up, give my best and work hard if I wanted to be a top money earner.

Then I thought about some of the top salespeople I knew that were making lots of money and having the time of their lives. I also remembered how much money I'd made and how much fun I'd had during the few times I was truly committed. I realized I enjoyed sales, and I felt there was nothing else that offered me the freedom, excitement and opportunity that sales did.

That was the day I made the decision that I was going to do whatever it took to be a top producer.

That was over 20 years ago, and I can still feel the power of that moment. I made a definite, conscious choice to get off the bench and into the game. I still had a lot to learn, but I decided I was willing to do whatever was necessary to make it to the top.

Over the next couple of years, I had many ups and downs, but for the most part, my sales career went extremely well. I learned a lot, won many awards and competitions, and achieved top honors as a salesperson. I was on the fast track to the top ... or so I thought.

"Our lives are a sum total of the choices we have made."
– Wayne Dyer

Eventually, the awards and honors weren't enough. I needed a new challenge, and I knew exactly what that challenge was: I wanted to start my own sales office. And not only did I want my own office, I wanted to build a team that could become number one in the nation. So I made a decision to do it.

At this point in my life, I was 20 years old. I had recently met my future bride, Susan, and she supported my decision. We set a date, made the arrangements, and with a lot of help and support, started our new office and our new life together. But after only a few months, I found out that running my own business wasn't as easy as I thought it would be. And to make matters worse, I wasn't working as hard as I should have been. I had gotten a little lazy and was trying to play "executive." In my mind, I had arrived.

Suddenly, we two newlyweds, with a new business and a baby on the way, found ourselves with no money and behind on our bills. For the first time since my "one sale, $100 month," I was struggling again. The reality of the situation didn't completely set in until my car disappeared. I thought it had been stolen, so I immediately called the police. The first thing they asked me was if I had made all the payments. It was only then that I realized my car had been repossessed!

> *"I never worry about action, but only inaction."*
> – Winston Churchill

This was another turning point in my life. I realized my success was determined by only one factor – me. As the saying goes, "If it is to be, it is up to me." So I made a decision to get my car back. I hocked some jewelry, used the cash to buy some inventory, borrowed a car, and went out that day and made three sales. Those three sales gave me enough money to get my car back and pay my rent for the month.

I learned some valuable lessons from that experience. **First, never think you've arrived. It's the surest way to the sidelines**. Second, when you make a decision and take action, you can change your life. Because I made a decision to get off the bench and take the initiative, I was able to turn a negative situation into something positive in one day's time.

Are you at a turning point in your life? Then make a clear, unequivocal decision to be the best and don't leave yourself any "outs." Tell yourself, "I'm going to do it. That's it. Period." The world is full of people who wish their lives were better but have never made the do-or-die decision that leads to superstardom.

You Gotta Take Action

Everything you have (or don't have) today is the result of the actions you've taken (or haven't taken) in the past. Taking action is like putting your car in gear. You can start the car and sit in it all day, but you'll never go anywhere unless you put it in gear and step on the gas.

We all have the option to take action and get off the bench and into the game, but most of us never do. Why? There are many reasons: fear of failure, fear of success, the perception of risk, "paralysis of analysis." The list goes on and on.

Some people won't take action because they're waiting for the "right" situation to present itself – waiting for another degree, the best time, the right opportunity, "things to get better," etc. They're looking for someone to hand them what they want instead of making it happen themselves. But success will never be handed to you. It takes a lot of hard work and effort. Just like with the car, you can wait for success, but you'll never achieve it unless you get in gear and take action.

Then there are people who feel that before they take action they have to analyze it, research it, think it over and discuss it with family and friends. Or people who think, "Someday, when I have more experience/learn more/become better, then I'll take action." Let me tell you, the road called "someday" leads to a town called "nowhere." These people will never get in the game!

Please don't get me wrong. Talking things over with other successful people is a good idea; analyzing an opportunity is important; learning is critical. But all the education, experience and advice in the world won't bring you success if you don't take action. There are many geniuses who don't have a dime because they never took action. Analysis sometimes equals paralysis. Don't get bogged down trying to figure it all out ahead of time. I've been in sales for more than half my life, and I'm still learning. Life is a constant learning and growing process. The important thing is to take action while you're learning, growing, stretching and becoming all that you were destined to be.

Perhaps the biggest reason people don't take action is a lack of confidence. Confidence is the feeling that you have what it takes to accomplish whatever task you set out to perform. We're all born with some degree of confidence, but as the years go by, our confidence gets squashed. We hear discouraging words like "no," "you can't," "you're too young," "you're too old," "you're too slow," "you're not smart enough," etc. And if we hear these negative words often enough, we can easily start using them when we talk to ourselves, hurting our confidence even more.

We also lose confidence as we face life's struggles and challenges —
personal relationship failures, business failures, bankruptcies, getting
fired or laid off, overcoming dysfunctional habits, failing to
achieve important goals, etc. Some of these situations are within
our control while others are not, but they can all negatively affect
our confidence. The bottom line is this: most adults struggle with
a lack of confidence every day.

So how can you regain this lost self-confidence? *You gotta* take
action! Here is a simple formula I use when teaching people how
to gain more confidence:

ACTION ⇨ RESULTS ⇨ SUCCESS ⇨ CONFIDENCE ⇨ ACTION

If you will just take action, eventually you will get some results.
Lots of positive results will give you some success. Success will
create more confidence. Greater confidence will lead to more
activity, and the cycle will continue. But it all starts with action.
Remember this: You don't have to be great to get started, but *you
gotta* get started if you're going to be great.

You Gotta Do It NOW

On a scale of 1 – 10 (1 being "things are utterly miserable" and
10 being "things couldn't be more wonderful"), most of us live
and perform at around 5 ("things are tolerable"). But 5 is probably
the worst place to be. Things aren't great, but they're not bad
enough to make a change either. Maybe we're only 20 pounds
overweight, or we sell just enough to get all the bills paid each
month. Our pain isn't great enough to force a change.

Then something happens that pushes us over the edge. We step on
the scales and discover we're 50 pounds overweight. Or the banker

calls to tell us we're $3,000 overdrawn on our checking account. We reach the point where we're fed up with the situation; enough is enough. We decide we're not going to live this way any more – not another day, not another minute. Have you ever had one of these moments in your life?

If you've had one of these turning points and you made the decision to change for the better, that's a great thing. But in the long run, that is *not* how we want to live our lives. That's living life in reaction. When you live in reaction, you're not in control of your life – life is in control of you.

Why do we put off doing the things we know we should do? Don't we usually have really good reasons? Unfortunately, all too often our reasons are just excuses. They're nothing more than stories we make up to justify to ourselves why we procrastinate.

My experience has been that people procrastinate for a number of reasons. We convince ourselves that the thing we have to do is "bigger" than it actually is. It's going to be too difficult, take too much time, cost too much money and resources, or require too much effort. Then there are fears and false beliefs that stop us from taking action. Salespeople often procrastinate to avoid rejection: "It's too far to drive … and even if I make the appointment, they probably won't buy anyway."

Perhaps the most common reason why we don't take action is because we don't think we have enough time. But in reality, it's rarely a time issue. It's a priority issue. We always find time for the things that are important to us.

Don't let excuses and circumstances dictate the quality of your life. You don't need a lot of complicated ideas to change your life. All you need is one idea that you will use. Take control of your life by taking action *now*. Now is what you can do this day, this hour, this moment to move your life forward. If you want to write a book, write one paragraph *now*. If you want to get in shape, go for a 10-minute walk *now*. You may not have an hour, but everyone has 10 minutes.

If you're in sales, get out of the chair and make a call *now*. If you can do that, you won't mind making a second, third or tenth call, and it will only be a matter of time before you achieve results and make some sales. Regardless of the activity, if you will consistently force yourself to take some kind of action *now*, the process will eventually become a habit and your success will increase.

Change is always initiated by a decision – a real decision that cuts you off from justifications and excuses. It may be scary, but you know in your heart it's what *you gotta* do. So make a decision today to move your life and your performance to a higher level. If you're at a 5, make a decision, develop a plan and take action now to move to a 6 and beyond.

To get in the game, move your attention to the immediate process of getting off the bench by making a decision and taking action.

Nike has a famous slogan that says, "Just do it." This simple statement is more profound than most people realize. It reveals one of the great keys to how life in general works. You have to just do it – no excuses. Even if you don't know how or you lack confidence, *you gotta* do it anyway … and *you gotta* do it *now*!

To get in the game, *you gotta* get off the bench.

To get off the bench, *you gotta*:

Make a decision;

Take action;

Do it *now*.

2 You Gotta Have a Dream

Although most of us will never **be star athletes** or win Olympic gold medals, *anyone* can be a star at the top of his or her own game. But to do that, *you gotta* have a dream. Having a dream is what drives you to get off the bench and get into the game. Dreams are goals; they are the targets you strive for that move you in the direction of your ultimate destination. Setting goals directs you toward the specific steps you need to take to succeed in life. Goals are also a means of "keeping score" so that you can determine if you're winning the game.

From all that I have seen time and time again, I've concluded that at least 90 percent of success derives from having a dream and knowing what you want. When I train others, the first thing I stress to them is to get a dream. If they already have one, they almost always need to redefine it and make it bigger. Then I teach them a simple but powerful pattern for achieving their dreams and goals.

> *"Most men die from the neck up at age 25 because they stop dreaming."*
> – Benjamin Franklin

You Gotta Know Where You're Going

People with dreams and goals succeed because of one primary reason: They know where they're going. Would you take off on an airplane if the pilot came over the PA system and said, "Hello, this is your captain. Welcome aboard. Today we're going to take off, fly in a random direction for a few hours, and eventually land … somewhere"? Of course you wouldn't!

> *"There is one quality that one must possess to win, and that is definiteness of purpose – the knowledge of what one wants and a burning desire to possess it."*
>
> – Napoleon Hill

Pilots must know their destination (their goal) and have a flight plan for every single flight. They understand that in order to arrive at a particular airport in a specified city at a designated time, they must fly at a specific speed, at a specific altitude and on a specific heading. They also know that as they fly the aircraft, they will have to make many small adjustments in order to stay on course and arrive at the correct destination.

The same is true for you. *You gotta* know where it is you want to go and have a plan or strategy for how you're going to get there. Otherwise, you could end up almost anywhere. If you stay focused on your goal, it will be easy to see the adjustments you need to make along the way to stay on course and achieve that goal.

You Gotta Define Success

In any game, you must determine what it means to win – *you gotta* define what success means to you. Each of us will have our own distinct definition of "winning" because we are unique in our individual dreams and aspirations.

In today's society, the popular definition of success is based on three major elements – power, money and fame. But this definition is narrow and excludes a multitude of people who are successful, yet define success by an entirely different set of standards. Consider the teacher who teaches values to a child. The child then grows up and lives a positive, productive life, where otherwise that same child might have taken a negative, self-destructive path. Or consider those who have dedicated their lives to causes such as visiting the elderly at nursing homes or providing food to the homeless.

Are these individuals any less successful than the quarterback who makes the game-winning play in the championship, or the CEO who turns his company around and takes it to the top? I think not; they just have different goals they're seeking to achieve. There are many people who are winning the game because they're living a life filled with purpose and realizing dreams based on their definition of success.

Take the time right now to think about what success means to you. One way to do that is to imagine yourself 5, 10, or even 20 years from now. Think about those things that, if you achieved them, would make you feel that your life had been purposeful and meaningful. Consider the following questions:

♦ What do you love doing?

♦ What are your values with respect to career, family, finances and health?

♦ How could you increase the quality of your life?

♦ How can you contribute to others in a meaningful way?

Once you're clear about your definition of success, you're ready to set the goals that will lead you to that success.

You Gotta Write Down Your Goals

I have found that the biggest mistake people make when working toward their dreams and goals is not writing them down. You may have thought a lot about your dreams and goals in the past, but if they're not written down, I'd be willing to bet you're not getting results. Just thinking about your dreams, even if you do it daily, isn't enough. If you truly want to achieve these things, *you gotta* get them on paper.

One person who taught me a lot about goals is the man who recruited me into sales, Gene Shelton. I learned firsthand from him how vital it is to actually write down your goals. At our weekly sales meetings, Gene would ask us for our goals, and I would tell him what I thought he wanted to hear. If someone gave Gene a goal, I always gave him a bigger one. I thought that was what goal setting was all about.

> *"Until you commit your goals to paper, you have intentions that are seeds without soil."*
> – Unknown

But Gene knew I wasn't writing them down because I wasn't getting results. So one day, he asked me to give him a list of the goals I wanted to accomplish professionally and personally in the next 10 years. This forced me to take time to think them through and write them down. As I did, my thinking started to change. I got excited, and I began to believe deep inside that I could actually accomplish them.

I gave Gene a copy of the list, and he sealed it in an envelope and put it away in a drawer. About five years later, he found that envelope and opened it. To our mutual surprise, every goal I had written down had been accomplished! The amazing thing about this story is, at the time I wrote those goals, I was living in a two-bedroom apartment, behind on my rent payments, and dead broke. Five years later, I had a new home, a new car and was financially free – and these were the exact goals I had written down and given to Gene.

This example shows the impact of writing down your goals – even if you forget about them. But the power of goal setting is not unique to my situation. According to Zig Ziglar, UCLA conducted a study on goal setting that focused on people who attended the Peter Lowe Success Seminars. The study included psychiatrists, truck drivers, civil service workers, salespeople and professors. Those with a balanced, written goals program earned twice as much as those without one: an average of $7,401 a month compared to $3,397 a month. The study also found that those with goals were happier, healthier and got along better with family members. Imagine the impact a consistent goal-setting program could have on your life, your family, your business and your finances!

Writing down your goals gives you clarity, and clarity is power. The clearer your goals are in your mind, the greater your chances of achieving them. When you write down your goals, they become embedded in a part of your brain called the Reticular Activating System (RAS). The RAS amplifies your thoughts and stimulates your ability to turn your goals into reality. It's like a filter that sifts out the things that don't pertain to your goals and brings into focus the things that do.

Here's an example of how the RAS works: Have you ever bought a car and then suddenly started seeing that kind of car everywhere? Those cars were always there, but you never noticed them because your mind filtered them out. But once you got that new car, your RAS brought into focus all the cars the looked just like yours.

According to Jim Madrid of Entelechy, the same thing happens when you write down your goals and read them daily – you stimulate the RAS and put it to work. Just like with the new car, your brain starts to notice anything that relates to the goals and dreams you have set. The RAS helps you say, do, act and react in ways that move you in the direction of those goals.

When you get your goals on paper, they become much more than just ideas – they start to materialize. The things you write down will be attracted to you – the right people, situations and opportunities will suddenly appear in your life. But if you don't have specific goals written down, then anything can be attracted to you, good or bad.

Do you have specific, definite goals, and are they written down? If you do, congratulations – you're in the game. If not, I'd be willing to bet you're not getting the results you want.

You Gotta Follow the Pattern

Dreams and goals give you a definiteness of purpose – they help you know where you're going. But they can do much more than that. For a salesperson, goal setting is without a doubt a primary indicator of income. In fact, those individuals in every walk of life who have clearly defined goals and dreams are the ones who consistently rise to the top and create extraordinary lives for themselves and their families.

As I mentioned previously in this chapter, early in my career I achieved great results from writing down my goals and dreams. That experience made me curious about the goal-setting process and how it works. So, I began to study everything I could find about goal setting and high-level achievement. I asked myself a few simple questions: Which strategies and techniques produce maximum results in the fastest time? How can these techniques be adjusted to make them simpler, easier to duplicate, and more fun?

Based on my research and experience, I developed a goal-setting pattern that represents the "best of the best." Using this pattern, I achieved incredible results with more speed and precision than I'd ever dreamed possible. I incorporated this pattern into a workbook called *The Dream Book* and started sharing it with my family, friends and business associates. Since then, *The Dream Book* has helped thousands of people improve their performance, produce accelerated change and change their lives.

The key to my goal-setting pattern is its simplicity. Many goal-setting processes are complex and cumbersome. The more complicated the process, the less likely it will be followed. Although there's not enough space here to share all the details of the pattern, following are the basic steps for accelerated goal achievement:

Step 1: Make a list of everything you want to achieve.
Consider all the areas of your business and personal lives, such as health and fitness, lifestyle, career, finances, relationships, and mental/spiritual issues. Let your imagination run wild. If you knew nothing was impossible, what would you attempt?

Step 2: Write down *why* you want to achieve these dreams and goals. Knowing your reasons will give you a sense of purpose. It will inspire you with the passion and power to make it through the inevitable challenges that come with pursuing your goals.

Step 3: Set a target date to achieve each goal. It has been said that goals are dreams with deadlines. Many people ask me, "What if I don't achieve a goal by the target date?" The answer is, "Set another date!" If you were building a skyscraper and didn't finish by the target date, you wouldn't quit! You'd simply set another target date and keep working.

Step 4: Get a plan. Set yourself up to win by developing an action plan for achieving your dreams and goals. Start with the ones you want to accomplish within one year and write down at least five things you can do to work toward each one. Keep it simple – people often make their plans so tough they become overwhelmed and give up.

Step 5: Take consistent action towards achieving your goals. If you're not doing something that moves you closer to your goals, you're actually moving backwards. Take small, steady steps that you know you can accomplish. Consistency is the key.

Step 6: Build your dreams. Go out and physically experience as many of your dreams and goals as possible. Take pictures and put them in a prominent place such as on your dashboard or bathroom mirror. Experiencing your dreams and goals firsthand makes them real for you in a way nothing else can.

In addition, I recommend reviewing your dreams and goals every day. As you read each one, imagine yourself achieving it. See it clearly in your mind's eye. Feel the joy and pride of accomplishment as you envision yourself attaining the goal.

And finally, as you achieve each dream or goal, replace it with a new, bigger one. Your first goals and dreams will take you as far as you can see; when you get *there*, you will be able to see even farther.

By now you're probably saying, "This is easy!" You're right! These six simple steps are the key to programming yourself to win. If you will follow the pattern and take action, you'll be well on your way to achieving extraordinary results. Soon your goals will become so important that physically and mentally you must achieve them. They will become a part of you and become your guidance system for life, sports, sales or anything else you dream of.

Always remember that dream building is an ongoing, life-changing process – a never-ending journey in which you can experience magic moments, consistent improvements and true success in every area of your life. Often times, you won't even realize that you're changing. But as you keep thinking about and internalizing your goals, you'll start to walk differently, talk differently and think differently. Your work ethic will improve, and you will become more positive about what you're doing. You'll begin to make the right moves with the right emotions, and you'll start getting results.

If you will set your goals, write them down, and take some kind of action every day, you will maximize your performance and build a solid foundation for an extraordinary life of achievement.

> *"Review your goals twice every day in order to be focused on achieving them."*
> – Les Brown

Take Goal Setting to the Next Level with
The Dream Book

If you are serious about success and winning, you can take goal setting to the next level by getting your own *Dream Book*. I originally developed *The Dream Book* as a way to help me set, manage and achieve my goals and dreams. It's one of the most advanced technologies for personal and professional achievement that I'm aware of, and yet the techniques are easy to understand and use. *The Dream Book* has been credited with helping thousands of people change their lives for the better. To order your own *Dream Book*, see the information page at the back of this book.

To win,
you gotta have a dream.

To get a dream, *you gotta*:

Know where you're going;

Define success;

Write down your goals;

Follow the pattern.

You Gotta Get the Competitive Advantage

If we're totally honest about it, most of us dreamed of being a star when we were young. We dreamed of making the winning shot, catching the "Hail Mary" pass, receiving the perfect score from the judges, or winning the pageant to become Miss America. Most kids on the playground dream of being in the championship game or winning a gold medal. Even kids who don't like sports still want to compete and win in music, the arts, scouting or the classroom.

From early childhood, competition plays an important role in our lives. You see, competition is what makes us better. It awakens the mind and activates the body, quickens the pulse and heightens awareness. When you are competing, everything else fades into the background and you become more focused. There seems to be a suspension of time – you are unaware of just how long you've been playing. And you begin to really care about the outcome.

> *"Of all the human powers operating in the affairs of mankind, none is greater than that of competition."*
> – Henry Clay

You can win some games just by being competitive. **But to consistently win long term and become a superstar, you gotta create and maintain a competitive advantage.** This distinct advantage is what allows you to consistently outperform the competition and put together a lasting winning streak.

Somehow, many people have come to believe that having a competitive advantage means disregarding the rules or cheating in some way. Nothing could be further from the truth. To gain an advantage takes hard work – you must do everything better than your competition does. You must challenge yourself and believe in yourself more than the competition does. And, *you gotta* want to win more than your competition does.

You Gotta Love a Good Challenge

To get the competitive advantage, *you gotta* love a good challenge. Mountain climbers aren't fascinated by molehills. They want the challenge of a harsh climate and thin air, of seemingly impossible heights. They accept that rocks fall, ropes fray, and muscles become weak and exhausted. That's what they love about it. They are eager to prove to themselves that they have what it takes to conquer the challenges and reach the top.

The same is true of top salespeople – they love a challenge. They're not interested in easy-to-achieve targets or quotas. They want goals that will make them stretch and grow; they want to be number one. They know there will be people who won't buy and sales that will be canceled along the way. They want to find out if they have what it takes to be the very best, no matter what challenges or unforeseen difficulties they might encounter.

The thing that is often so unsatisfying about our careers (and many times, our lives) is not that the success we desire is too hard to attain. In fact, it's the opposite. It's that we have lowered the standards that define success, and we expect success to be easy and predictable. As a result, we feel unchallenged and rather empty.

But when we seek challenges – take on new responsibilities, tackle the projects and tasks that no one else will do – it is then that we start to rise above the crowd and climb ever higher into the thin air of real success. We need to realize it is only the biggest challenges that are worthy of our best efforts.

> *"There is no passion to be found in playing small – in settling for a life that is less than what you are capable of living."*
> – Nelson Mandela

You Gotta Create a Burning Desire

Athletes and teams don't win championships unless each individual wants to win so fiercely that he or she would do just about anything to make it happen. The same is true for each of us – if we're going to win our "championship," we have to be willing to do whatever it takes. We must find, and nurture, that burning desire to win.

Deep inside most of us, there has always been a desire to win. Unfortunately, many people lose that desire somewhere along the way. Maybe they've faced so many failures they've convinced themselves they will never win. Or perhaps they just don't have enough reasons to get motivated. The more reasons you have to achieve something, the more desire, inspiration and motivation you will create inside of you.

I've never played a game that I didn't want to win. It is this intrinsic desire for competition that attracted me to sales. And yet, there's a big difference between just wanting to win and having a burning desire to win. I know, because I didn't always have a burning desire to rise to the top of my profession. And let me tell you, it makes all the difference in the world.

Do you remember the story about my car being repossessed? Well, just a few weeks after that, I had the opportunity to attend our company's national sales convention with my wife. However, at this point in my career, I was on the bottom, couldn't afford to go, and didn't understand the value of attending meetings and training events. So, we missed the first day and didn't think anything of it.

I will never know exactly why, but the second day, I woke up before dawn and decided we were going to that meeting. Susan thought I was crazy because the meeting was a four-hour drive away, and we wouldn't arrive until noon. But it didn't matter; I had made a decision and we went.

Although we were only there for the second half of the second day, attending this meeting had a profound impact on my life. There were featured speakers and top achievers from across the nation. I don't remember who the presenters were, but I will never forget one statement made by one of the top money-earners in the country: "Set yourself on fire, and people will gather to watch you burn." I didn't really understand what he meant, but it was a catchy phrase that stuck in my mind.

Later that evening, we attended the awards banquet where the top producers received bonuses and recognition for a job well done.

What I especially noticed was the excitement, emotion, attitude and pride the winners had about their success. Their actions, and the atmosphere at this event, reminded me of something you would experience at an Olympic awards ceremony. These high-performance individuals had that "in the gut" burning desire to win. I realized this was the same drive that star athletes (or anyone else who achieves incredible success) must have to make it to the very top of their games. It was then I understood that these top performers were "on fire." They absolutely radiated success, motivation and passion. It didn't matter if they were 18 years old or 80; they had a burning desire to win, and people gathered to watch the glow.

Although I had felt this burning desire to win in sports, I had never experienced it with my sales career. I realized that if I was going to achieve my full potential, I had to find a way to dig deep inside and ignite this passion. And that's what I did! I discovered that when you want something – I mean really, really want it – there is an internal reaction that goes off inside you that says, "YES!" The energy that is released in that moment of desire creates one of the most powerful and magnetic forces in the universe.

> *"Winning isn't everything, but wanting to win is."*
> – Vince Lombardi

Throughout the years, I've worked with thousands of people from every walk of life, and one of the questions I am asked on a consistent basis is, "How do I get this burning desire to win?"

The key is to find that one thing you want so desperately that you would be willing to move Heaven and Earth to get it. Ask yourself,

"Of all my dreams and goals, which one is most important …
what do I want more than anything in the world?" Stop right now
and jot down your answer.

Now that you've discovered your heart's desire, write down all the
reasons why this one thing is so important to you. Think about
what it will feel like when you achieve this dream. If you get
enough emotional reasons, you will create the burning desire
you need to make it happen.

You Gotta Believe You Can Win

As Susan and I drove home from that convention, I evaluated our
situation. How could I take my struggling team and make it
number one in the country? I thought back to my days as an athlete
in high school – how did we win games? Then I thought about all
the winning teams I had ever seen or read about. That's when I
realized that all successful athletes and winning teams have a
game plan – a strategy for success. I realized I had to develop a
game plan for our team.

As I continued driving home, all I could think about was developing
a strategy that would take our small team to number one. Everything
else seemed to fade into the darkness of the winding road. As we
approached a small town, a bright neon sign in front of a bank
startled me. In big bold letters that seemed to shout at me, the sign
said: "Success begins with CAN. Failure begins with CAN'T."

I took out a notepad and wrote down the words from that sign.
Then I wrote down my goal to be the top rookie dealer in the
country and the steps we would have to take to accomplish that
goal. I decided there was no such thing as "can't" and no such
word as "impossible." At the time, I only intuitively understood

the power of the words "can" and "can't." Now I know that whichever one you consistently tell yourself becomes a self-fulfilling prophecy.

By the time we made it home at 2:00 a.m., I was so excited I couldn't sleep. I had "the burn." Every fiber of my being knew this was the time to go for it. All I had to do was follow the game plan, most of which I had just learned at the convention. I was so convinced we could be number one that I started writing the acceptance speech I would give at the following year's convention when our team would win the top rookie dealer trophy.

From that point on, our team became competitive, and we began to believe we could win. As a result, our sales started to explode. At the next convention, our team members were the ones who were on fire and winning the awards. My office was the top rookie dealership in the nation, and I was asked to give a speech. As you might have guessed, I gave the speech I had written the year before in the middle of the night. The first words I said were: "Success begins with CAN. Failure begins with CAN'T."

> *"If I believe I can't do something, it makes me incapable of doing it. But, when I believe I can, then I acquire the ability to do it even if I do not have the ability in the beginning."*
>
> – Mahatma Ghandi

What a difference a year can make if you just decide to get in the game and believe you CAN win!

You Gotta Make It a Game

If you're playing to win, *you gotta* make whatever you're doing a "game." Games promote competition, and competition challenges you to rise to levels you have never reached before.

Imagine that you're at a football game. Just before the running back is about to cross the goal line for a touchdown, he stops running, lays the ball on the ground and walks off the field. Now, that would never happen. Maybe it would in practice, but the fact that it's a game makes us want to beat the competition. It makes us care more about winning.

It's relatively easy to make sales a game because most sales organizations inherently understand the power of the game concept. That is why they create contests, bonuses and awards. I've always noticed that, in sales, the people who work to win the contests and achieve the awards always make the money. Why? Because of the competition. Most people will work harder for awards and recognition than for money because of the satisfaction they get from beating the competition and winning the game. Every salesperson who has ever told me the awards and recognition didn't mean anything was not being honest with himself.

To really make sales a game for our organization, we created an atmosphere where people felt like they were part of a team, where they were given the opportunity to win, and which made them want to compete. To accomplish this, we simply incorporated a few of the elements that exist within a game or contest. For example, we "kept score" by tracking everyone's progress and constantly updating our "scoreboard" so that everyone could see who was winning the game.

Having a scoreboard is an essential element of any game. By constantly showing the score, it helps you know where you're at, evaluate your performance, and make the adjustments necessary to win. In our organization, the scoreboard was a marker board and some simple charts and graphs that showed key information for every salesperson, including sales goals, the number of prospects seen, and closing ratio. Everyone was able to see how he or she compared to other salespeople; and as a team, we were able to determine whether we were winning. Salespeople were challenged to set goals, to compete with each other, and to outperform the competition.

I've used this same type of scoreboard system to help organizations and individuals increase their performance and achieve record results. Regardless of your career or endeavor, you can incorporate elements of a game to encourage healthy competition. You can create a competitive environment in virtually any profession and provide a reward for almost every situation. (For example, if you accomplish a personal goal, the reward can be as simple as buying something you've been wanting or celebrating with dinner at a special restaurant with your spouse.) I encourage you to develop a scoreboard. All you have to do is determine the top three or four criteria for success for your particular endeavor and then track your results for those criteria.

When everyone competes, everyone wins. The company wins because it increases productivity, results and profits. The top performer wins and receives the awards and recognition he or she desires. Even those individuals who don't achieve top honors win because they almost always achieve more than they would have if they hadn't competed.

Competition encourages us to do our best, and ultimately, that is what determines who the real winners are. If you know in your heart that you've given your all and put forth your best effort, then you'll always win no matter what the scoreboard says.

Decide to be a competitor. Leave it all on the playing field. Always accept the biggest challenges and give them your best efforts. Dig deep inside and rekindle your burning desire to win. Pick out other individuals who are doing more than you and make it your goal to be better than them. But most of all, compete with yourself. Every day, commit to being better than you were the day before. That's how you get the competitive advantage that will take you to the top.

To win,
you gotta get the competitive advantage.

To get the competitive advantage, *you gotta*:

Love a good challenge;
Create a burning desire;
Believe you can win;
Make it a game.

4 You Gotta Play the Numbers

The power of numbers is the basic philosophy of the most successful businesses. Sam Walton built the Wal-Mart Empire on the power of numbers – he developed a profitable working model and then duplicated that model over and over again. He knew that more stores meant more sales, more sales meant more profit, more profit meant more capital to build more stores, and the cycle continued. Today, Wal-Mart is the world's largest retailer.

Even athletes have learned to use the power of numbers to their advantage. The star athlete is not always the one with the most talent; but many times he will score the most points – usually because he takes the most shots. The top athletes know that winning is a numbers game – the more shots you take, the more opportunities you have to score.

Interestingly, the person who makes the most shots is almost always the person who misses the most. In 1927, Babe Ruth set the single-season home run record with 60 home runs. That same year, he also led the league in strikeouts with 189. Likewise, Cy

Young won more games in his pitching career (511) than anyone else in the history of baseball. He also lost more games (316) than anyone has ever lost. And yet, which records are both men remembered for?

I would rather have an average salesperson who is willing to "play the numbers" than a superstar who never takes any shots. The salesperson that plays the numbers will always have more opportunities to close more sales.

If you want to win, *you gotta* play the numbers. Fortunately, you can learn how to leverage the power of numbers in everything you do. The key is to find a basic pattern or model that is simple, proven and duplicatable. Many businesses already have successful models, so you don't have to figure out what works and what doesn't. And many personal goals you might want to achieve – such as losing weight, getting in shape, earning a degree, or paying off debt – also have proven success patterns. All you have to do is discover and learn the success model for whatever it is you want to achieve and then repeat it on a mass scale to achieve predictable results.

You Gotta Learn and Practice the Basics

To use the power of numbers, *you gotta* start by learning the basics – the skills and knowledge that are critical to your success. Then *you gotta* practice them over and over and over again until they become habit. Many Olympic champions train at least eight hours a day, six or seven days a week. They practice the basics repeatedly, day in and day out, and that's what makes them champions.

When Michael Jordan was in the tenth grade, he was cut from his high school varsity basketball team. The next morning, he got up and started practicing. He practiced constantly. He shot thousands and thousands of baskets. Sometimes he made it and sometimes he missed; but he kept shooting because he had a burning desire to get back on that team.

The next season, he made varsity and led the team to the state championship. After high school, he played at the University of North Carolina, and as a freshman, scored the game-winning shot for the national championship. Michael went on to make many more game-winning shots and eventually won six NBA championships. It's not surprising that he also made the shot that won his final championship. Clearly, Michael could make the shot when it counted the most. He always went back to the basics and made the same shot he had made in practice thousands of times before.

The same principles can be applied outside of sports. When I got into sales, I had minimal knowledge and lacked confidence. But because of my competitive nature, I wanted to compete with the better, more experienced salespeople – the superstars of the company. I quickly realized that to get better I needed to learn and practice the basics.

In sales, the basics are prospecting, presenting, listening, asking the right questions and closing. No matter what your career or endeavor – accountant, writer, manager, teacher, parent, student, etc. – there are basic skills that are necessary for success. If you're a parent, some of the basics are telling your children, "I love you" and teaching them respect by having them say, "Yes, ma'am" and "No, sir." If you're a student,

> *"Success is nothing more than a few simple disciplines, practiced every day."*
> – Jim Rohn

the basics are attending class, reading for comprehension, taking notes, and studying.

Whatever your game is, find out what the highest achievers in your field are doing and how they're doing it, and then mimic their techniques. This is called "modeling": If you do the same things that successful people do, in the same manner, with the same attitude, beliefs and emotion, you will get the same results. I didn't understand that modeling was such a powerful concept early in my life, but now I consistently practice it in every area where I want to improve.

I learned the basics of sales and public speaking by watching the videos and listening to the audios of the top salespeople and the most sought-after speakers. I practiced my presentations in front of a mirror with the same tone, the same gestures and the same intensity as these individuals. I videotaped myself to determine which areas needed improvement, and then I practiced those skills and techniques more.

Make a habit of reading the books, listening to the audios, attending the meetings and networking with the successful individuals in your area of interest. Once you've learned the basics, you need to get good at executing them. The only way to do that is – you guessed it – practice! Then practice some more! Eventually, you will master the techniques, and they will become a natural part of you.

Even the most successful individuals can improve their performance if they get better at the basics. Tiger Woods has been hitting golf balls since he was a toddler, and practicing the basics remains a crucial part of his daily routine. The will to win is the will to prepare and practice, practice, practice.

You Gotta Use the Power of Numbers

Whether you're a salesperson, business owner, teacher, or someone who wants to lose weight and get in shape, it's vital that you know your averages and use them to achieve results. One of the amazing things about statistics involving people is that, individually, they are unpredictable; yet in total, they are very reliable. So once you understand how the law of averages works, you can use it to generate predictable results simply by playing the numbers.

Here's an example of how it works: If you are a salesperson, and on average, for every 20 people you see 5 buy, then your closing ratio is 25 percent. Once you know your average, it's easy to determine what you have to do to achieve a certain goal. If your goal is to close 50 sales, you know you need to get in front of 200 people. It is true that you will never know which 5 out of 20 people will buy; but if you understand the law of averages, you don't give up if the first 5 don't buy or even the first 15 don't buy!

Salespeople often ask me how they can increase their income. I explain to them that the fastest way to increase their income is to increase the number of qualified prospects they spend time with. Even if everything else stays the same (your skills, your averages, etc.), if you will double the number of qualified prospects you see, you will double your sales income.

The real power of these principles happens when you combine the law of averages with massive numbers. I learned that early in my sales career. I understood that as long as I had a decent closing percentage, I didn't have to be the best in any particular area in order to be number one. All I had to do was know my averages, set a goal and then play the numbers. I've used these same principles throughout my career for recruiting, training and managing my businesses and their profits.

The truly great thing about knowing your averages and playing the numbers is that even if you're inexperienced or have less-developed skills, you can still produce just as much or more than the superstars who may have a better average than you do. For instance, a salesperson who closes 5 sales for every 20 presentations given (a 25 percent closing ratio) can sell just as much as a person who closes 5 out of 10 (a 50 percent closing ratio). All the person with a 5/20 average has to do is see 20 people for every 10 people the 5/10 salesperson sees. Of course, the salesperson with the 5/20 average has to give more presentations – that's why it's a numbers game.

Understanding these principles gives you confidence and power. If you're in a slump in your business or life, you can always get out of it quickly by knowing your averages and playing the numbers.

You Gotta Evaluate Your Performance to Improve Your Averages

A professional baseball player always knows his averages because the difference between batting .250 and .300 can mean millions of dollars each year. Can you imagine making that kind of money for being just five percent better? A few percentage points can mean the difference between being average and being a superstar, between sitting on the bench in the minor leagues and starting in the major leagues.

It's the same in business and in everyday life. I like to say, "The weight of a petal of a rose often determines which way a decision goes." In other words, the small things can make a huge difference. Improving your averages by even a small percentage can mean the difference between just getting by and getting rich.

Think about it. Suppose you're in sales and your average is 5 out of 10 sales, and you see just 10 people each week. If you were to improve your average to 6 out of 10 – close just one more sale each week – you would make 52 more sales every year. If you multiply 52 by your average commission per sale, you can see the tremendous impact of improving your average! If your business had 10 salespeople and all of them improved their averages by just one sale per week, it would mean 520 more sales per year. Do you see the advantage?

Improving your averages really means improving your performance, and you can improve your performance no matter what you do. Let's assume you're a teacher. Perhaps the average you use to gauge your success is your students' standardized test scores. If you could take steps to improve their test scores by 5 percent, what impact would that have on the students and on you? Would you win an award for teacher of the year? Playing the numbers could mean improving students' test scores by 5 percent for every class you teach, year after year after year. Imagine how many students' lives you could profoundly affect!

You can improve any average or result by constantly evaluating your performance and making adjustments. Start by asking yourself these simple questions:

1. What are some areas I want to improve?

2. Which areas, if improved, would have the biggest impact on my career/life?

3. What are some simple steps I can take daily to become better in these areas?

When it's all said and done, one of the very best ways to improve your performance is to get more experience; and nothing gives you more experience and confidence than actual "game time." If you're in sales, "game time" is the time you spend in front of qualified prospects. The more you do anything, the better you will get at it. You just gotta get in the game and take a whole lot of shots. When you miss, make some adjustments and then take some more shots. Remember: a missed shot is not a failure; it's an opportunity to move one step closer to the perfect shot.

You Gotta Be Consistent

To achieve long-term success, *you gotta* consistently play the numbers in all areas of your life. If you're only nice to others occasionally, it's unlikely that you will win many friends or influence many people. If you only contact new prospects once or twice a month, you're never going to be a top producer. If you only buy one piece of real estate, chances are you're not going to become a successful real estate developer.

Walt Disney was told "No" by virtually every person he talked to. They said his idea of a cartoon about a mouse was absolutely ridiculous. As a matter of fact, he was turned down by 302 bankers before he found someone that would fund his vision. Stop and just imagine the loss that millions of children and adults around the world would have experienced if Walt Disney had not believed in his vision enough to keep playing the numbers.

You will never achieve anything of great significance if you're not willing to consistently play the numbers. The Good Book says, "Ask and it shall be given to you." But it goes a bit further by saying, "Seek and ye shall find" and "Knock and it shall be opened unto you." This is a powerful principle for success in

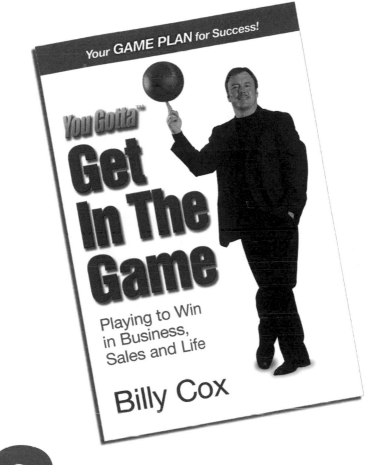

Your GAME PLAN for Success!

You Gotta™

Get In The Game

Playing to Win
in Business,
Sales and Life

Billy Cox

3 Easy Ways to Order Copies for Your Sales Team!

1. Complete the order form on back and fax to **972-274-2884**

2. Visit **www.CornerStoneLeadership.com**

3. Call **1-888-789-LEAD (5323)**

CornerStone
Leadership Institute

☑ YES! Please send me extra copies of *You Gotta Get In The Game*!
1-30 copies $14.95   31-100 copies $13.95   100+ copies $12.95

You Gotta Get In The Game	____ copies X ____ = $ ____
You Gotta Get In The Game Audio CD set	____ sets X $19.95 = $ ____
The Dream Book	____ copies X $14.95 = $ ____
Making The Dream Book Work Audio CD set	____ sets X $19.95 = $ ____
Playing In The Majors Audio CD	____ copies X $ 9.95 = $ ____

Additional Sales & Customer Service Resources

Sales & Customer Service Package   ____ packs X $129.95   = $ ____

Other Books

_____   ____ copies X ____   = $ ____

_____   ____ copies X ____   = $ ____

_____   ____ copies X ____   = $ ____

Shipping & Handling $ ____

Subtotal $ ____

Sales Tax (8.25%-TX Only) $ ____

Total (U.S. Dollars Only) $ ____

Shipping and Handling Charges

Total $ Amount	Up to $49	$50-$99	$100-$249	$250-$1199	$1200-$2999	$3000+
Charge	$6	$9	$16	$30	$80	$125

Name _____ Job Title _____

Organization _____ Phone _____

Shipping Address _____ Fax _____

Billing Address _____ Email _____

City _____ State _____ ZIP _____

❑ Please invoice (Orders over $200) Purchase Order Number (if applicable) _____

Charge Your Order: ❑ MasterCard   ❑ Visa   ❑ American Express

Credit Card Number _____ Exp. Date _____

Signature _____

❑ Check Enclosed (Payable to: CornerStone Leadership)

Fax 972.274.2884
Phone 888.789.5323   www.**CornerStoneLeadership**.com   **P.O. Box 764087**
Dallas, TX 75376

anything you do. Think about it: If you consistently *ask* enough people, if you are constantly *seeking* out new opportunities, and if you are willing to *knock* on enough doors, then eventually doors will *open*, you will *find* the right opportunities, and you will be *given* the results you desire.

Remember, winning is all in the numbers: Practicing the numbers, improving the numbers, and consistently playing the numbers.

To win,
you gotta play the numbers.

To play the numbers,
you gotta:

Learn and practice the basics;

Use the power of numbers;

Evaluate your performance to improve your averages;

Be consistent.

5 You Gotta Think Like a Winner

Early in my sales career, I was invited to a training seminar several hours from home. I decided to attend and caught a ride with an associate named Ken. Ken was an experienced salesman, doing a great job and making lots of money. I was a young rookie who asked a lot of questions. I could tell Ken got tired of answering my questions, but I kept asking because I was eager to learn.

Eventually, he threw me a book and said, "Read it." The book was *Think and Grow Rich* by Napoleon Hill. As I read that book, I began to understand that we become what we spend the most time thinking about. Then I remembered what the Good Book says: "As a man thinks in his heart, so is he." This concept, that we become what we think about most often, is actually one of the foundational concepts of most religious and philosophical beliefs. Our thoughts determine our actions, our moods, our self-image, even the words we speak. We can change our situation in life

"Winners are those people who make a habit of doing the things losers are uncomfortable doing."

– Ed Foreman

simply by changing the way we think. In short, ***our thoughts determine our destiny***. You are today where your thoughts have brought you. You will be tomorrow where your thoughts take you.

I wanted to be a winner, and I realized I had to start thinking like a winner. Although I had achieved some results, I knew I needed to change my thinking if I was going to achieve the kind of success I really desired. So I began to diligently study success principles by reading hundreds of books, constantly listening to audios, and attending seminars and training led by some of the world's leading experts in success and high performance. I discovered there is one distinctive trait that all winners have: They know that success is a mental game – they understand the power of positive thoughts.

If you want to win your game, *you gotta* think like a winner. And you must use both defensive and offensive strategies. Defense is about protecting yourself, and guarding your mind against negativity should be your number one defensive strategy. Offense is about getting results. Offensive strategies for winning include visualizing success, controlling your attitude and expecting victory.

You Gotta Guard Your Mind

You can give 100 percent day and night, but unless you guard your mind, it's unlikely you will live up to your full potential. That's because there is a constant battle going on in your mind between positive and negative thoughts. Remember, you will become what you think about most of the time. If you make the mistake of dwelling on negative thoughts, you're going to end up being someone and somewhere you don't want to be. The consequences of negative thinking are the destruction of your dreams and giving up everything you've worked for.

In our society, too many people are out of shape mentally. Most people have never learned how to control their thoughts. As a result, they don't have the desire or the strength to choose positive thoughts and eliminate or replace negative ones. When our mental muscles are weak, we are easily swayed by the influences, opinions, and ideas of others.

There are two main sources of negativity that continually assault our minds and thoughts:

♦ **Our environment** – Outside influences feed us negative information virtually all day long. Did you know Americans watch an average of *seven hours of TV a day*? And if they're not in front of the TV, they're probably reading the newspaper, listening to the radio or checking the latest gossip magazines. Consider this: News has to sell. What sells better – positive or negative news?

Unfortunately, most of us are also surrounded by pessimistic people – family members, peers, business associates, even people we casually come in contact with in stores and restaurants. Most of these people aren't negative intentionally; they're just affected by the same negative environment we are. However, that doesn't change the fact that if we constantly listen to negative, depressed people, we will become negative and depressed.

♦ **Self-destructive thoughts** – Too many people believe that their past equals their future. In other words, they think that their past failures and disappointments will continue and that they'll never achieve the success they desire. Much of our negative self-talk comes from bad experiences we had growing up. Perhaps someone said something hurtful to us, or we chastised ourselves for not meeting our own expectations. If we allow ourselves to continue this harmful self-talk that goes on in our heads, our thinking becomes a self-fulfilling prophecy. If we think thoughts of defeat and mediocrity, we will live a defeated life.

Most people aren't aware of how negative their thinking really is and how many of their thoughts are self-destructive. Try this quick exercise: For just one hour, jot down every thought that pops into your head, every comment you make to yourself, and every judgment you make about yourself. At the end of the hour, tally up how many are negative and how many are positive. Unless you already practice positive-thinking techniques, I can virtually guarantee that the self-destructive thoughts will far outnumber the encouraging ones.

To guard against all this negativity, *you gotta* get in shape mentally. If you don't defend yourself against negative influences, you'll wind up drained on the sidelines of life. You must train your mind and develop the mental muscle and the will to resist the negativity that comes at you from all directions. Condition yourself to think positively, or you'll go back to the pessimistic state of mind most people live in. If you don't control your mind, it will control you.

Here are just a few steps you can take to guard your mind:

1. **See things as they are.** Do a mental checkup to make sure you have a true and clear picture of reality. It's easy to be lulled into thinking things are worse than they really are. Ninety-five percent of the things we worry about never happen, and the ones that do happen are never quite as bad

as we imagined they would be. When you consistently see things as worse than they are, you become overwhelmed and discouraged.

2. **Be aware of your thoughts.** Are they positive and uplifting or negative and destructive? Consistently ask yourself, "Is this the type of thinking that empowers me and builds me up, or discourages me and makes me weak?" Self-awareness is the first step to making a change.

3. **Get rid of any negative thoughts immediately.** It only takes a little bit of poison to kill success. Cancel negative thoughts by saying the words, "Cancel, cancel."

4. **Replace negative thoughts with positive ones.** Keep your mind strong by feeding it positive thoughts of success. Anyone can find problems. If you want to be a top achiever, choose to find the positive in every situation. You'll find it if you look hard enough.

If you will practice these skills every day, eventually they will become habits, and you will literally reshape the quality of your life.

You Gotta Visualize Success

Almost all superstars understand and practice the concept of visualization. Professional and Olympic athletes include visualization techniques in their practice schedules. They set their goals and then visualize themselves achieving those goals over and over again in their minds. All else being equal, these top performers know that winning is a mental issue. The better prepared they are mentally, the better they will perform when it really counts.

Who can forget Mary Lou Retton in the 1984 Olympics? The pressure was on for her to win the gold, and she needed a perfect score of 10.0 on the vault. She had visualized herself flawlessly performing her routine literally hundreds of times before. When the time came to do it for real, her body was able to execute the routine perfectly. What the mind can conceive, the body can achieve. She became the first American woman to win the gold medal in the all-around individual gymnastics competition.

> *"Visualization*
>
> *lets you*
>
> *concentrate*
>
> *on all the*
>
> *positive aspects*
>
> *of your game."*
>
> – Curtis Strange

Visualization involves repeatedly imagining a scene or goal with intense clarity and feeling. It goes beyond just reading your goals and dreams to purposefully visualizing yourself achieving them. Vivid mental pictures are as real to your subconscious mind as actual experiences. Your physical body and subconscious mind can't tell the difference between something that actually happens to you and something you vividly imagine is happening to you. That's why a football coach will take video footage of a player, edit it to show only the very best plays, and then have the player watch it. Repeatedly seeing himself at peak performance levels sends a powerful message to the player's subconscious mind about his capabilities. The result is an actual improvement in the player's performance on the field.

Visualization works in more than just sports – it's effective in any area of your life where you want to improve your performance. I learned years ago to use the power of visualization and applied it to my sales career. For 12 years I ran a sales office. In 10 of those years, our office was either number one or two in the nation. Our team never had fewer than 5 of the top 20 salespeople in the company; and three different times we had the number one salesperson in the world. The secret to our success was that each salesperson developed goals and then regularly visualized himself achieving them.

Top-notch business people routinely rehearse their presentations in their minds. Legendary motivational speaker Zig Ziglar says he usually spends two to three hours mentally preparing before he gives a speech, even though it may be one he's given many times before. His goal is to give a fantastic speech that exceeds expectations, and he knows mental preparation improves results.

The key to visualization is to not merely think about your goals and dreams, but also to see, feel and touch them in your mind's eye. Feel your success or the completion of your goal with strong emotions. Find a quiet time, close your eyes, and mentally picture the things you want to happen as if they were real and happening to you in the present.

If you want to be a champion salesperson, *you gotta* spend dedicated time mentally preparing. Always take a few minutes prior to each sales call or presentation to visualize each step of the process. If you can, pull over to the side of the road and relax for a few minutes. Get a clear, vivid picture in your mind of the specific outcome or results you desire. This will help you get in the right mental state to win.

If a task or goal seems impossible to accomplish, it's because you're only using the conscious, mechanical part of your mind. Visualization taps into the spiritual, subconscious part of your mind and unleashes the incredible power that comes from absolute inner certainty. When the big sale needs to be closed, when you need a 10.0 to win and performance is a must, there will be no doubt in your mind that you will succeed.

You Gotta Control Your Attitude

To think like a winner, *you gotta* learn to control your attitude each and every day. It all starts with you. You are the CEO of You, Incorporated. Jack Welch, the former head of General Electric, summed up the truth about attitude when he said, "Nothing of any importance has ever been accomplished by a pessimist."

Most people just don't understand that your attitude can be your best friend or your worst enemy. It can take you to levels you never thought possible, or it can be the single most limiting element in your life. Your attitude – good or bad – is contagious. It spreads to others you come in contact with – your family, your friends, your coworkers. It affects everything you do.

Having a bad attitude will cost you sales, business, friends, time and energy. You will never make it to the top of your game if you consistently have "stinkin' thinkin'." Of course, everyone has bad days and gets depressed once in a while. However, if you learn to control your attitude, your consistent thoughts and beliefs will always prevail.

When you have a good attitude, good things happen. The adage that success is 90 percent attitude and 10 percent aptitude is true. I've always noticed that the salespeople with the best attitudes sell more. All superstars have a super attitude. They absolutely refuse to major in the minors or let little things get them down.

Having a good attitude is a deliberate, conscious choice, and making a choice starts with knowing where your attitude is every day. Consciously analyze your attitude – give yourself a checkup from the neck up. Ask yourself, "How is my attitude today? Is it great, bad or just okay?" If the answer is "bad" or "okay," what can you do to change your attitude? Think about what has caused your attitude to slip. Is it just the normal negatives of life or is there something unusual or major going on?

Next, determine if this is a situation you can control. If it is, take the steps necessary to get the situation back on track (one of which is working on your attitude). Even if you can't do anything to improve the situation, the one thing you can always do is learn something from it and control your attitude.

Whether your attitude is great, bad or just okay, you should work to improve it every day. If you don't reinforce a positive attitude, it will turn negative over time. Just as an athlete's muscles will become weak if he or she doesn't exercise them, your attitude will deteriorate if you don't take proper care of it. Here are some things you can do to control your attitude:

- Read positive books.

- Listen to motivational audios.

- Visualize your goals every day.

- Associate with positive people.

- View every situation as a challenge or an opportunity for improvement.

You Gotta Expect Victory

Do you wake up in the morning thinking, "This is going to be a lousy day" or "Nothing good ever happens to me"? If you're in sales, and you have an important presentation to make, do you tell yourself, "I don't have a chance at closing this sale"? If you routinely think this way, how does your day turn out? Do you make the sale? I'd be willing to bet you get exactly the results you expected.

Winners wake up every morning with excitement, enthusiasm and confidence, knowing that success is in store for them. Winners set their minds for victory; they set their minds for success.

Setting your mind for success doesn't happen automatically. You have to constantly tell yourself that today is going to be a great day, good things are going to happen and doors are going to open for you. Go out each and every day believing success will come your way.

Now, you may be thinking, "Billy, I've got so many problems. My marriage is in trouble, my business isn't doing well, nobody will buy from me, and my health is going downhill. How can I live with enthusiasm? How can I be positive when I have so many problems?"

You gotta make a decision that you're going to have confident expectancy about everything you do. You have to continually expect that things are going to get better. Expectation is a conscious choice to use the habit of faith. It is a conscious choice to see a positive outcome instead of a negative one. As you think, so it is created. As you believe, so it is done.

Expectancy is about seeing beyond where you are. Look out through your eyes of faith and see yourself happy, healthy, enthusiastic and successful. See things better than they are ... see them as you want them to be. Develop a habit of focusing on what's right in your world instead of what's wrong, on what you have instead of what you don't have.

You're probably asking, "What if I do that and it doesn't work?" Then you haven't lost anything.

My question to you is, "What if you do it and it works?"

If you will consistently think about and focus on what you want, you will ultimately get it. By focusing on positive thoughts, you open up your mind to start attracting success in all areas of your personal and business life. This is why top salespeople seem to effortlessly sell so much more than average negative-thinking salespeople. People want to do business with positive, upbeat, successful individuals.

"A competitor will find a way to win. Competitors take bad breaks and use them to drive themselves just that much harder. Quitters take bad breaks and use them as reasons to give up."
– Nancy Lopez

When things look impossible or you're tempted to go through the day negative and depressed, that is when you have to step up and change your belief level. Expect good things to happen. Expect to rise above your challenges. Expect victory!

When those around you are predicting doom and gloom for everything from the economy to your goals and dreams, remember that success is mostly a mental game. Your thoughts will drive your results, your success, even your destiny. So defend your mind against the negative, proactively focus on the positive, and expect victory. You have the power to choose your thoughts and your attitude and therefore, your success.

To win,
you gotta think like a winner.

To think like a winner,
you gotta:

Guard your mind;
Visualize success;
Control your attitude;
Expect victory.

Formula for Thinking Like a Winner

If you change your **thoughts**…
>> you will change your *beliefs*.

If you change your **beliefs**…
>> you will change your *expectations*.

If you change your **expectations**…
>> you will change your *attitude*.

If you change your **attitude**…
>> you will change your *behavior*.

If you change your **behavior**…
>> you will change your *performance*.

If you change your **performance**…
>> you will change your *life*.

You Gotta Be Coachable

W hile your skills and your willingness to work hard are important, you will succeed much faster if you are coachable. Being coachable means you are willing to listen to, take advice from, and learn from those who have more experience than you do. If you are coachable, you can learn virtually all of the skills you need to win the game.

One of the greatest things a coach can say about a player is that he or she is coachable. Teachers love to find students who are eager to learn. Sales managers get excited when they find trainees who are eager to grow in the organization. Unfortunately, too many people are "hot shots" – they feel as if they are invincible and already know all the strategies for success. As a result, they won't listen to people who have more experience and wisdom than they do.

"It marks a big step in your development when you come to realize that other people can help you do a better job than you could do alone."

– Andrew Carnegie

There is an old adage that says: "Learn from the mistakes of others, because life isn't long enough to make them all yourself."

You Gotta Listen So You Can Learn

Listening is a critical part of your long-term success. If you don't listen, you can't learn. And if you want to earn more, *you gotta* learn more. Tony Robbins says, "If you do what you've always done, you'll get what you've always gotten."

Continuous learning is the key to superstardom. The highest-paid professionals in any field spend more money improving themselves than the average individuals who just get by. This means they are constantly listening to self-improvement audio programs, listening to top performers at seminars, and "listening" to the wisdom found in books.

> *"He that won't be counseled can't be helped."*
> – Benjamin Franklin

If you are willing to listen, you will learn what works and, just as importantly, what doesn't work. Take advantage of the wisdom of your coaches, teachers, peers and mentors – it will help you avoid costly mistakes and unnecessary setbacks.

I see many top salespeople join a sales force and start out with a bang. The ideas and techniques they use work well, and they achieve some initial success. Then, somewhere along the way, they start to think success is easy. They stop listening, and they find ways to cut corners. Many of them don't even realize they've changed, but the shortcuts eventually catch up with them and they fall into a slump. This is the time when they must refocus, get back to the basics, quit taking shortcuts and start listening to their coach.

There will be many ideas and techniques you may want to try throughout your career that have already been tried, tested and shown to fail. Your coach can guide you safely past these landmines, but *you gotta* listen. If you don't, you could do great damage to yourself and possibly to others by spending too much time, energy and effort in areas that will lead to certain failure. I learned that lesson the hard way.

One of my biggest challenges in sales management occurred shortly after I was promoted to sales director. Things were going incredibly well. We had just achieved the status of number one sales team in the world, and I had promoted five of our top salespeople to opening their own offices. Things couldn't have been better … or so I thought!

While attending my first directors' meeting, I discovered that I was being undermined by one of the top producers I had promoted. He was going behind my back telling others in the company that he was the reason for my team's success and that without him our team wouldn't survive. I had a choice to make: I could try to solve this problem on my own, or I could listen to the advice and wisdom of the other directors. I chose to listen and learn.

At that meeting, I received a lot of good advice and some constructive criticism. The other directors let me know I actually had quite a few problems in my organization and that I had many challenges ahead of me. They also told me it probably wasn't the smartest move to have promoted my top five salespeople all in the same year. I learned that I needed to stay in closer contact with the people in my organization and to keep my ear to the ground. Because my peers were kind enough to share personal experiences about how they overcame similar challenges – and because I was willing to listen and learn – I went home with some different strategies and a new plan to take our organization to the next level.

That year I worked harder and smarter than ever before. I invested more time, effort and energy into the individuals in our organization. The team saw that I was willing to be coached and knew without a doubt that I was in the game. Because of that, I earned their support. That year we were able to once again become number one, and we broke three long-standing production records – all without the salespeople I had promoted the year before.

The moral of the story is this: I went to that first directors' meeting feeling a little invincible. I was a 22-year-old rookie making incredible money and living life to its fullest. Because I was on top, I could have easily let my ego get in the way and not listened to the older, more experienced directors. Instead, I did listen and turned lemons into lemonade and gained invaluable experience. I think I also earned the respect of my colleagues, not only as someone who would listen, but also as someone who would take action based on the advice he had been given. In short, I proved I was coachable.

The failures I've experienced in my career have taught me that each level of success requires more commitment and a willingness to listen more and learn more. There is no such thing as "arriving" or "making it." Many people have a good year, and suddenly you can't tell them anything. I'm always disappointed to see that happen because it's a condition that will eventually send them back to the starting gates.

You Gotta Have the Right Coach
Any superstar athlete will tell you that *you gotta* find the right

coach. Studies have shown that having the right coach or mentor can make all the difference in your performance. If I were in the computer industry, I would want Bill Gates or Michael Dell as my mentor and coach. I would want to tap into the knowledge and wisdom that got them to the top of their game.

You can, and should, do the same thing. Every avenue of life has its superstars. Seek them out. Spend time with them and ask them questions. Find out how they became so successful. Pick their brains and learn their pattern or model for success. Get to know how they think and what makes them "tick." The reality is this: if you ask the right people the right questions, you will get the right answers. These relationships can offer you a wealth of knowledge and the opportunity to improve yourself by implementing the same strategies that have made others so successful.

You may be wondering how to find the right coach. There are people in your life who can be great mentors for you. My first recommendation is that you have different mentors and coaches for the different aspects of your life. Each individual will have unique talents and skills that you will want to emulate. Some of them may have the attributes you admire in physical health and vitality. Some might be experts in marketing and management, while others have exceptional interpersonal skills.

> *"Learn from the legends, watch the top players, and apply tactics that work for them to your own game."*
> – Brad Gilbert

Find those individuals who are the highest performers in the area you're interested in. You don't want counsel from someone who's only been involved in that endeavor for a year or two. Seek out individuals whom you admire and respect and can relate to. When considering whether someone is the right coach for you, ask yourself the following questions:

♦ Is this someone I am willing to tell my commitments to?

♦ Is this someone I would share my failures and successes with?

♦ Is this someone that will lead me by example and someone I will follow?

♦ Will this person hold me to a higher standard and not let me off the hook?

♦ Will I follow through with this person even if it is uncomfortable or difficult?

Take time now to write down the names of three to five individuals you know (or would like to know) who possess the characteristics you want in a coach. Even if you don't know them, write them down for two reasons. First, if you're willing to work hard enough, you can meet anyone on the planet you want to meet. You may have heard of the theory of Six Degrees of Separation. The concept (which has been tested and proven) is that anyone on Earth can be connected to any other person through a chain of acquaintances that has between five and seven links. But even if you can't meet the person, there are likely numerous sources of information (articles, books, audios, seminars, websites) by or about them that you can access. Use these sources to study their attitudes, work habits and belief systems and then duplicate them.

Many people have asked me how they should ask someone to become their mentor. My answer is, "You shouldn't."

First and foremost, having a mentor is an internal decision on your part. It's about being open to observing and learning from others. The external part of coaching involves seeking out individuals you want to emulate and then gradually establishing a relationship with them. Don't go up to someone you barely know and ask them to become your mentor and spend a lot of time helping you. Instead, over a period of time, ask them questions about themselves and how they became successful. This will help you develop some rapport. Eventually you will feel the time is right to ask them if they will share some of their strategies for success with you.

I do have one warning for you when it comes to finding the right coach: Be careful whom you associate with and listen to. Find successful mentors you can look up to that will guide you. Now you might think that's obvious, but you would be surprised how many people take advice from mediocre performers or from family and friends who don't have "the fruit on the tree." Every time I attend a meeting or seminar I see the same thing: A top salesperson is on stage giving advice about how he or she achieved success. I walk out into the hall and see a group of people in the corner, and the person who has sold the least is giving everyone else advice on how to sell! This is the same person who has bill collectors calling, has four bald tires on his car, and is selling less today than he was five years ago. It always amazes me that there are people who are willing to listen to him.

> *"Remember: We become who we spend time with. The quality of a person's life is most often a direct reflection of the expectations of their peer group. Choose your friends well."*
> – Anthony Robbins

If you were to ask me what I feel has been the single most important thing that has helped me throughout my career, my answer would be simply, "I am coachable." Almost everything I know about sales and life in general I have learned from mentors and coaches, whether I got it from spending time with the person or indirectly from books or audios. I understand there are people who know a lot more than I do, and I'm always anxious to discover what it is.

Even if you're successful and winning the game, you still need to be coachable and listen to and learn from people with a proven track record. In Michael Jordan's book *For the Love of the Game*, he makes a comment regarding the idea that he was the greatest basketball player of all time: "I built my talents on the shoulders of someone else's talents … I have used all the great players who came before me to improve my skills … I listened, I was aware of my success, but I never stopped trying to get better." He was able to achieve truly unprecedented success by learning from those who had achieved success before him. If it worked for Michael Jordan, it can work for you.

To win,
you gotta be coachable.

To be coachable, *you gotta*:

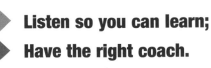

Listen so you can learn;
Have the right coach.

You Gotta Sell Yourself

Whether we realize it or not, everyone is selling something. The teacher sells the students on making good grades and getting an education. The preacher sells the congregation on attending church and receiving salvation. Parents sell their children on being good citizens. And kids are always selling their parents on something they want. To see this in action, just tell a kid, "No" and watch the "sales campaign" begin!

If you want to win and achieve your full potential in life, *you gotta* sell … whether you're in sales or not. Your entire life is a continuous process of communicating, persuading and influencing other people. Tony Jeary is known as the world's

> *"Everyone lives by selling something."*
> – Robert Louis Stevenson

utmost authority on speaking and presentations. In his book *Life Is a Series of Presentations*, he convincingly states that the average person makes hundreds of presentations a day. Anytime you communicate with someone – whether it's in business or at home, via email or face-to-face – you're making a presentation. And each of these presentations can have an impact on your life and future. I think anytime you make a presentation, you're trying to sell someone on something, even if it's as simple as selling someone on your idea or opinion.

Even athletes sell. A star athlete sells style, skills and showmanship. Through his performance, he sells people on the idea that he is the best, and because of this, he creates great excitement. Because he is recognized as a winner, people want to buy the products he endorses and tickets to watch him play. But a star athlete must also continually sell himself *to himself* in order to consistently perform at the highest level. If the superstar's confidence slips, he loses his edge and his performance suffers.

Selling yourself is a critical factor that determines the level of success you will ultimately achieve and how quickly you will achieve it. Regardless of your profession or personal interests, you should be networking, marketing yourself and getting your name "out there." When you promote yourself to others (in an appropriate way), more opportunities will come your way and you'll have better "luck." Of course, it won't be luck at all. Good things will happen to you because people will be aware of you and your abilities. When companies downsize, who typically stays? The people who have marketed themselves, their results and their value to the company. Selling yourself is a universal need.

Selling yourself involves two things: First, it means selling others on you and your products or services. But it also means selling you *to you*. You've got to believe 100% in yourself, your abilities, and whatever it is you represent. How can you sell others on you if you're not first sold on yourself? I'm not talking about having a big ego. I'm talking about being totally convinced that you are the best person for the job or that the person you're exchanging with is getting a good deal. To sell to others, *you gotta* be sold on yourself.

You Gotta Believe

Selling in its most basic form is only a transfer of belief. It's sharing what you wholeheartedly believe with others and letting them share in your belief and excitement.

How is it that two people selling the same product, for the same company, in the same territory, working the same hours, can consistently get significantly different results? It's because one person has a strong belief in his abilities and his product, and the other one doesn't.

All superstars believe they're going to be successful. They believe it with their minds and their hearts. When Michael Jordan was in a game, do you think he believed he was going to miss his next shot? How about Tiger Woods: When he's at the tee, does he believe he's going to slice the ball? No way. He has no doubt in his mind he's going to make the perfect shot every single time. Of course, not every shot is "all net" or a hole-in-one, but the person who combines skill with belief usually succeeds.

When top salespeople make a sales call, they never say, "I might sell something today" or "I hope someone buys." Instead, they say, "I know someone is going to buy what I'm selling today. I have a product/opportunity/service I believe in. The prospects have money, and I'm going to trade my belief and enthusiasm for their money."

If you wanted to sell your boss on the idea of giving you a raise, would you know without a shadow of a doubt that you're worth every penny? Or would you feel lucky if you got anything because you don't think you deserve it? If you expect to achieve great things, *you gotta* believe 100 percent in you!

I'm not a psychologist or a neuroscientist; however, both my research and my personal experiences have shown me that our beliefs about ourselves can actually manifest in physical reality. Your belief dictates your behavior. If you believe you will succeed, you will. If you believe you will fail, then failure is certain. What you believe to be true about yourself is rendered true because of the link between your belief and your actions.

When you have a strong enough belief in yourself, you will release the positive power of belief and transfer that belief to others in a very natural way. As a result, you will dramatically improve your chances of achieving the outcome you desire.

You Gotta Ride for the Brand

I strongly believe that anyone who represents a product, service, company or organization must be loyal to that product, service, company or organization. Years ago, when cowboys worked on ranches, they called this "riding for the brand." Each ranch had its own brand, such as "Bar 2" or "101." But the brand was more than just a way to mark cattle. It symbolized the ranch and the qualities that ranch represented, and it also symbolized the cowboys as individuals. The cowboys were fiercely loyal and committed to their brand and were willing to stand up for it.

In professional sports, many athletes have sponsors. That is the brand they represent, and they are expected to use and be loyal to that company's products and services. If Tiger Woods were a spokesperson for a certain brand of golf balls, he should use their balls exclusively. What would people have thought if Michael

Jordan promoted Nike shoes but played in Reeboks? He would have lost credibility with buyers and most likely his endorsement contract with Nike.

In sales, riding for the brand goes much deeper than just being loyal to the products or services. *You gotta* also be loyal to your company, your customers and yourself. You should never represent or sell anything to anyone unless you truly believe customers are making the best choice by spending their hard-earned money to purchase your product. How can you be convinced customers are getting the best deal if you haven't spent your own money to buy and use the product? Would you expect to become a top Ford car salesman if you drove a Chevrolet?

> *"Loyalty is something you give regardless of what you get back. In giving loyalty, you're getting more loyalty; and out of loyalty flow other great qualities."*
> – Charlie "Tremendous" Jones

Let's pose that question from the buyer's perspective: Would you buy a Ford if you looked over and saw the salesperson's Chevrolet sitting in the parking lot? Probably not. You'd think, "If this salesperson doesn't think a Ford is good enough to drive, why should I buy one?"

The concept of riding for the brand is applicable to just about everything you do. It's about being loyal to and supporting your family, friends, church, or alma mater. I've never seen anyone make it to the top who wasn't completely loyal to the products, services, organization, idea, philosophy or cause he represents. Why would you waste your time and energy on something you don't or can't believe in?

If you don't believe in and support the causes you're involved with, you're being a hypocrite, and it will be evident to everyone else. You shouldn't ask other people to do something you won't do. You can fake it for a while, but you won't reach your highest potential as long as you're pretending. Riding for the brand is still the only way to gain lasting credibility.

You Gotta Create Win/Win Situations

It's easy to be enthusiastic when you represent a product, service or cause that creates a win/win situation for everyone involved. When a sale is made, the salesperson always gets a win – he makes a commission. With that commission, he creates a certain lifestyle for himself and his family.

But to create a win/win, the customer must also win. The win for the customer should be that they've acquired a useful or valuable product or service – something that saves them time or money or offers peace of mind and safety. If you want to consistently be a top producer, you should strive to give each customer a bigger win than the one you receive. In other words, long after you've spent your commission, the customer should still be receiving the benefits of the product or service.

Creating win/win situations is really about giving a little more than you expect to receive. Ask any marriage counselor and he or she will tell you that to have a great marriage, you've got to give more than you receive. When you volunteer for a charity, your church or your community, you give your time, effort, energy, and money. What you get back is the feeling that you've made a significant impact on the lives of other people.

Look for the win/win situation in everything you do. Then work to make it happen. It's not hard to get excited about representing something if you know the other party always wins because of your efforts.

You Gotta Love What You Do

When I made the decision to stick it out in sales, financial reasons were not the determining factors. My decision was made through careful evaluation of what I liked – and didn't like – about this kind of work. I found that sales is the best profession for me because there are more things about it that I like than dislike. I love the fact that I have the opportunity to meet so many different people. I also love that I can set my own hours, determine my income and have unlimited potential to advance. To me, sales means freedom!

To achieve the highest level of success and perform at your peak ability, *you gotta* love what you do. Otherwise, you will become easily sidetracked. You won't stick with it through the inevitable tough times, and you won't be willing to consistently do the things necessary to succeed.

> *"Selling is essentially a transfer of feelings."*
> – Zig Ziglar

If you don't love what you do, you have two choices: You can either change what you do, or you can change what you love. Often times, you'll be better off figuring out what you love about what you do than changing careers. Why? Because no matter what you do, you'll always be able to find something you don't like about it.

I once read a story about Benjamin Franklin. It said that Franklin made decisions by taking a piece of paper and writing all the reasons to do something on one side and all the reasons not to do it on the other. Then he would evaluate both sides and make his decision based on the results.

I challenge you to do the same. Take a sheet of paper and draw a line down the middle. On one side, write everything you love about your career, hobby, volunteer job, etc. Then, on the other side, write everything you don't like. Now, evaluate both sides. Most of the time, you will find more things that you like than dislike. But you can't just look at the number of reasons on each side – you also have to evaluate the relative meaning and impact of each reason. For example, you might have three positives and five negatives. But the three positives may be huge, quality-of-life issues, whereas the five negatives are minor administrative headaches you could learn to live with.

This exercise will help you discover what motivates and excites you. When you focus on the positives, the negatives will become insignificant. And as you focus on the things you like, you will love what you are doing even more. The more you love what you do, the more you win.

If you come to the realization that you truly don't like what you do or that you can't live with the negatives, you need to start looking for an exit strategy. Find something you do love, and I'd be willing to bet you'll be successful at it.

Remember, the most important sale you'll ever make is to sell yourself on who you are and what you do. You will be the toughest prospect you'll ever have. If you can sell *you*, you've got it made.

To win,
you gotta sell yourself.

To sell yourself, *you gotta*:

Believe;

Ride for the brand;

Create win/win situations;

Love what you do.

8 *You Gotta* Raise the Bar

I've spent my entire career raising my personal bar higher and higher. It began with learning how to sell, then becoming a top salesperson, and then recruiting and managing people. With each step came the opportunity to challenge myself and stretch my comfort zone.

There is an old saying that states, "By the mile it's a trial; by the yard it's hard; but by the inch it's a cinch." You can raise your bar by taking one small step at a time. Every time you succeed, consider what it took to get there. Evaluate what worked and what didn't. Then *you gotta* raise the bar again by setting a new, bigger goal to shoot for. Once you raise the bar to new heights, it's unlikely your performance will fall to its former level.

> *"Unless you try to do something beyond what you have mastered, you will never grow."*
> – C.R. Lawton

You Gotta Go the Extra Mile

Part of raising the bar is going the extra mile – giving a little more, doing better than your best. Many people say, "I can't give any more than I'm already giving" or "That's the best I can do." I say they're wrong.

In his book, *Leading from the Lockers*, John Maxwell shares the story of the first man to run a mile in under four minutes. For years, athletes had tried to break this seemingly unbreakable time barrier; experts said the human heart would explode under the conditions necessary to run a sub-four-minute mile. However, on May 6, 1954, Roger Bannister did it. He ran a mile in 3 minutes, 59 seconds.

> *"The man who can drive himself further once the effort gets painful is the man who will win. The principle is competing against yourself. It's about self-improvement, about being better than you were the day before."*
>
> – Steve Young

There are two amazing aspects to this story. The first is that Roger Bannister wasn't a professional runner. In fact, he was a medical student who set aside only 45 minutes a day to train. But he refused to believe that it couldn't be done. In his mind, there were no limits. When asked how he did it, his reply was simple and profound: "It's the ability to take more out of yourself than you've got."

The other fascinating thing about this story is that by setting a new world record, Roger Bannister changed the sport of running forever. Within two months of Roger's achievement, John Landy set a new sub-four-minute-mile record. The next year, 37 other runners broke the four-minute mile. Since Roger Bannister first set the record in 1954, hundreds of runners have run a mile in under four minutes.

So what happened? There were no great breakthroughs in training; no one discovered how to control wind resistance; human bone structure and lung power didn't suddenly improve. What happened was that someone – someone not that different from you and me – made a decision to give just a little more than he thought he had. Someone decided that he could do better than his best. Once he proved it could be done, the bar was raised for everyone else.

Never accept the idea that there's a limit to how far you can go. It's your responsibility to shatter this type of thinking, explore the realm of the untested, and discover breakthrough opportunities. There's a quote by Joel Barker I keep on my mirror that says, "Those who say it can't be done are usually interrupted by others doing it."

Each of us has had times when we've tapped into that something extra, that something that pushed us beyond our limitations. You can tap into this reserve more consistently by stretching yourself a little bit every day. That's what Roger Bannister did. He worked to improve his speed every day – sometimes by only milliseconds. But over the years, the constant stretching paid off.

Most of us want to just hop on an elevator, push a button and quickly arrive at success. Instead, you have to improve one level at a time; you need to construct a "stairway to success." The most your mind will accept is a small improvement over your last accomplishment. If your best effort produced 10 sales in one week, your next goal should be 11 sales in a week. If you rode the exercise bike for 20 minutes today, shoot for 21 minutes tomorrow.

My father taught me a lesson when I was very young that has remained with me throughout my life: "Good, better, best; never let it rest, until your good is better and your better is best." We can't jump directly from "good" to "best." Instead, there are countless steps of "better" and "better still" until we finally reach a world-class performance level.

If you're in sales, you can go the extra mile by making just one more contact before lunch. On your way home, follow up on a few leads. Each day, call on one client you've lost or haven't sold to in a while. Just say hello and remind them you're still there if they need anything.

You can use the same idea to raise the bar in other areas of your life. Regardless of the activity, always reach and strive for the next level and never settle for less than your very best. By raising the bar of your personal expectations every day, you will achieve things you never thought possible.

You Gotta Get the Mental Edge

I know a lot of salespeople with average talents and abilities who are multimillionaires. I also know a lot of very talented salespeople who are broke and in debt. What's the difference? The multimillionaires understand the importance of having a "mental edge."

> *"Change your thoughts and you can change your world."*
>
> – Dr. Norman Vincent Peale

How well you perform involves much more than the sum of your talents, skills, abilities and experience. Strong mental preparation is often the difference between the winners and the also-rans. Elite athletes know the truth behind the adage, "Winning is 90% mental and 10% physical." In fact, many of them believe that having a mental edge is so important, they hire sport psychologists or performance experts to help them get it and keep it.

If you want to be an elite performer, *you gotta* learn how to develop a mental edge. Then you must be willing to do what it takes to stay in top mental shape. Developing your mind is a lot like developing your body. First, you have to identify the areas you want to improve, like getting rid of a belly and love handles or toning your arms and shoulders. Then you have to establish *and follow* a training regimen to eliminate the flab and strengthen and build the muscles. You can get your mind in shape by following the same steps. So let's get started. (Before continuing, get a notepad and six 3x5 index cards.)

Step 1: Identify Areas to Improve

Let's start with your mental problem areas – the mind games that hold you back and keep you from performing at your peak ability. Some examples are fears, limiting or false beliefs, doubts about yourself and your abilities, destructive self-talk, etc. Perhaps you have a negative attitude about something or someone on your team. Maybe you're overwhelmed by the fear of giving a presentation or asking for the order. Or perhaps it's a lack of motivation and discipline. If you can identify and eliminate these problem areas, you will gain the critical mental edge.

On the notepad, write down all the areas you can think of that need improvement. Now, from this list, pick the three that represent your biggest obstacles to success. Write each one at the top of a 3x5 index card.

Now let's look at your existing strengths. These are qualities, characteristics, behaviors and actions that contribute to your success. Go back to your notepad and write down all the strengths you can think of. We all have strengths – plenty of them – and there's tremendous value in knowing what they are.

From your list of strengths, pick the three that, if you improved them to the next level, would have the biggest impact on your success. Write each one at the top of a 3x5 index card.

Step 2: Establish a Training Regimen

Training your mind is just like training your body. Exercising and lifting weights gets rid of fat and strengthens your muscles. Creating and reading affirmations eliminates your problem areas and strengthens your strengths. An affirmation is a positive statement about you. It describes specific traits or characteristics you want to develop or the type of person you want to be. Effective affirmations are stated:

- ♦ In the present tense, using the word "am" instead of "will be";

- ♦ In the positive, without using words such as "not" or "don't";

- ♦ In the first person, using the words "I" and "my";

- ♦ In concise and clear terms – they are short and specific;

- ♦ With action-oriented phrases that begin with the words "because" or "by" – these phrases describe the actions you are willing to take to make change possible.

For each of the three problem areas you identified, you're going to develop a positive affirmation. For example, an affirmation for a basketball player struggling with free throws could be:

"Because of my perfect form and spectacular shooting skills, I am a consistent 70 percent free-throw shooter." If your problem area is really big, your affirmation should represent a small step toward eliminating it.

Here are some examples of common problem areas and affirmations for salespeople:

- ♦ Fear of contacting prospects: "Because I work my leads as if they are gold, I have more than enough prospects to see each and every day."

- ♦ Poor work habits: "Because I understand the importance of hard work and discipline, I am a self-motivated person who has an excellent work ethic."

- ♦ Problems with presenting and closing: "Because of my strong ability to present and close, I consistently close over 70 percent of the prospects I see."

For each problem area, write the affirmation on the applicable index card. Then, completely erase or mark through the problem at the top of the card so that you can't read it any more. (This is the first step in getting rid of your old negative habits.)

Now go back and develop a positive affirmation that will enhance each of your three strengths. Write each affirmation on the applicable index card. Below are some examples of strengthening affirmations. (Fill in the blanks with *your own* particular strengths.)

- ♦ Because I am committed to studying the latest strategies and techniques, I am constantly improving my ___*communication*___ skills.

♦ I raise the bar daily in all areas of my performance in
   sales and marketing by _staying focused and
   committed to my goals and dreams_ .

♦ I am an exceptionally talented _manager_ who
   demands more of myself than others expect of me.

♦ I stay ahead of the competition by making my good
   better and my better best.

Step 3: Follow the Training Regimen

As with any fitness plan, if you don't follow it, you won't see
any changes. The same is true of your mental fitness plan. *You
gotta* follow the plan and exercise your mind every single day.
Read all your affirmations daily along with your goals,
especially in the morning (when you awaken or on your way
to work) and in the evening before going to sleep.

For the best results, read them out loud and with commitment
and emotion. Speaking your affirmations is more than a mental
workout; it's also an emotional workout. It sends a message to
your brain that you mean it. When you positively affirm
something with emotion on a consistent basis you stimulate
the RAS in your brain to open up your mind to the possibilities
of your success. **You truly can speak things into existence.**

At this point you're probably saying, "Billy, you're crazy.
You're telling me to talk to myself out loud? People are going
to think I'm nuts!" My response would be, "Aren't your goals
and dreams worth feeling a little nuts?" I hope your answer is,
"Yes!" But the good news is you can actually make it fun. With
modern technology, people will simply think you're talking
on your cell phone hands-free, especially if you do your
affirmations in the car. Just look over, smile and keep affirming!

I've never known anyone who consistently spoke his or her affirmations out loud, engaging the body and emotions with total belief, that did not have a total life transformation. I promise that you will see a dramatic impact on your performance if all you do is speak your affirmations for five minutes each day before work. It will make a noticeable impact in your attitude, your thinking and how people respond to you each day.

By reading your affirmations daily, you will develop a mental edge by overcoming your problem areas and strengthening your strengths. And, as with exercise, the more you do your affirmations, the faster you'll see results. It's all about repetition and consistency.

Follow these simple steps, and you will develop the mental edge that will take you to the top of your game.

You Gotta Have Discipline

Raising the bar takes discipline ... and lots of it. Even among athletes who have exceptional physical abilities, surprisingly few have the self-discipline required to hone their skills to a razor's edge and become true superstars. A well-disciplined athlete is one who attends every practice, works to sharpen skills and is careful about things like diet and sleep habits. As a result, each day he is able to push just a little bit beyond the previous level.

Likewise, a well-disciplined salesperson is willing to make the number of calls required to get the appointments he needs, makes every appointment on time, follows up with each prospect and fulfills the promises he makes. The successful salesperson does these things whether he feels like it or not – even if it's Friday afternoon and he'd rather be playing golf.

An essential ingredient to success in any area of life is learning to discipline yourself. You already have the ability to succeed in any endeavor you choose. The question is, do you have the self-discipline needed to develop that ability to its full potential? By applying the same principles of discipline that superstar athletes use to your unique talents and abilities, your chances of winning will increase significantly.

> *"Discipline is the habit of taking consistent action until one can perform with unconscious competence. Discipline weighs ounces, but regret weighs tons."*
>
> – June Rhee

In fact, you have a much better chance of achieving success than an athlete does. Did you know that the odds of a high school football player making it to the NFL are 4,000 to 1? Or that only 5 to 6 percent of baseball players drafted will ever play in the major leagues?

As a culture, we are not conditioned to discipline ourselves. The word discipline comes with a negative connotation. Some people view discipline as a lack of freedom. I believe discipline equals freedom because you know that you're in charge. If you tell yourself you'll do something, you do it. You know you will follow through with your commitments.

There is really no such thing as a totally undisciplined person, even though that term is often used. You will always be disciplined – you can either choose to discipline yourself or life will do it for you. It is far better to choose the former. The "school of hard knocks" will leave you battered and bruised, while self-discipline will make you prepared and powerful.

Evangelist and former pro baseball player Billy Sunday has a speech titled "Payday Someday." Its basic message is that someday you will either receive a great reward or have to pay a great debt. That's the way it works in athletics, business or life – your efforts will eventually pay off or your lack of effort will eventually cost you dearly.

You can raise the bar in almost every area of your life. **What if you spent just 15 minutes a day on self-improvement? Where would you be in a year, two years, five years or even a lifetime?** Consistently raising the bar isn't easy. It will take tremendous courage, dedication, and a lot of hard work. But you can do it. Learn how to push yourself. Then, every day, push yourself just a little further. Every day, expect just a little bit more from yourself. Look for tangible or measurable improvements. Then you'll begin to realize that you are giving a little more, and you will know you have raised your own bar to new heights. That's what makes it fun!

To win,
you gotta raise the bar.

To raise the bar, *you gotta*:

Go the extra mile;

Get the mental edge;

Have discipline.

9 You Gotta Have a Team

To win in any game takes **teamwork.** Even athletes in individual sports are part of a team. Every successful boxer has a trainer, a manager, a sponsor and a gym. A victorious racecar driver needs a pit crew, a sponsor and an owner. World-class gymnasts have trainers.

No matter what you want to accomplish in life, it will be virtually impossible to achieve superstar status unless you work with a team. You don't win championships by yourself. Life is a team sport. You will need the help and support of others to reach your goals. To win in sales, you need a team – a good company behind you, a dedicated service department and an effective leader. Even personal goals like losing weight or quitting smoking are more easily attained when you have a team around you. Your spouse, parents, children, siblings, friends, and neighbors are all part of your support network. They can keep you on track and lend encouragement during tough times.

"Coming together is a beginning; keeping together is progress; working together is success."

– Henry Ford

Chances are, Michael Jordan would not have achieved such long-term, spectacular fame without a team of winners around him. His team made him better, and in turn, he made them better. He passed off many game-winning shots to his teammates; but because his team won, he won. A great player needs a great team just as much as a great team needs great players.

You Gotta Be a Team Player

To win consistently, *you gotta* be a team player. What does it mean to be a team player? It means communicating and cooperating with others. It's about being patient and being open to the ideas of other people, even people who may be very different from you. Team players are solution oriented – they help create win/win situations for everybody involved. And team players share leadership responsibilities and accountabilities.

> *"One person seeking glory doesn't accomplish much. Success is a result of people pulling together to meet common goals."*
>
> – John Maxwell

Notice how the word "team" is spelled. There is no "I" in "team." When I am on a team, I have to learn how to blend in and work with others. I am not self-centered or interested only in results that meet my personal objectives. In some ways, I must lose my "self" and my selfishness as I come together with others to achieve something I could not achieve on my own. Now look at the word "win." There is an "I" right in the middle of "win." **With a team around me, I can win!**

Notice that the "I" stands between the "w" and the "n." There is no "win" without all three working together.

When you're part of a team, your individual goals become subservient to the team's objectives. We see this mentality throughout successful businesses, sports teams and perhaps most clearly in the military. Everyone has a specialty and a particular mission or job assignment. The overall success of a military operation is dependent upon the successful completion of hundreds of individual missions.

Team players know that being on a team is a two-way street. You see, a team will only be successful if every team member is willing to give and take. If you want to receive support from others, you have to give support. If people are there just to get, it never works. Always keep in mind Zig Ziglar's famous saying from his book *See You at the Top*: "You can get anything you want if you help enough other people get what they want."

I believe that to be totally fulfilled in our professional and personal lives, we must be connected to others and contribute to their success and well being. I've always heard that if you go to the top of Success Mountain by yourself, you'll probably jump off.

You Gotta Know Your Role

An essential part of being a team player and helping your team win is knowing what role or position you're expected to play. As you learn to adapt to each role and become successful at it, your role on the team will change. As time goes by, the role you play will become bigger and more important.

> *"None of us is more important than the rest of us."*
> – Ray Kroc

When I started in sales, I knew nothing about it, so it would have been silly for me to try to create my own team. Fortunately, I was able to join a winning team and contribute to its success. As my skills and confidence increased, so did my role, and I became a bigger part of the team. Over the years, as I gained valuable experience and knowledge, I began to assume various leadership duties. Eventually, I became President and Chief Operating Officer of the company. Obviously, there is no way I could have started out at this level. I had to start with small roles and work my way up to larger ones. At each point along the way, I knew I had a certain position to play in order for the team to be successful. I took each role seriously, had pride in my position and worked hard.

Just as in sports, there aren't always enough positions for everyone on the team to play the position he or she wants. Some people aren't willing to accept the role the coach wants them to play. They don't realize the coach understands the bigger, long-term picture and has the best interests of the team in mind. As a result, their negativity creates disharmony on the team. People who aren't willing to play the position the team needs them to play will eventually be replaced.

Sometimes you're better off playing a role that's different than the one you want. You may be asked to play a role you don't even feel you're good at, but you have to realize you've been given this role for a reason. Frequently, taking on a different position or project can be a tremendous boost to your career.

No matter what position you're asked to play, give it your all. Know that you're contributing in a very important way to the overall success of the team. Remember: When the team wins, you win.

You Gotta Be a Little "Political"

Let's face it – if you're involved in any group or team, you're
going to have to deal with some amount of politics. That's just the
way it is. But if you're aware of the political elements in any given
situation, your success will bloom at a faster rate.

I know a lot of people who never seem to get anywhere in life. They
often talk negatively about their company or their teammates, and
they don't buy into their company's philosophy, vision or leadership.
This is their downfall because their leader and company can never
rely on them. They don't realize they are their own worst enemy.

To be successful, *you gotta* publicly support your team's mission
and stand behind your leader and teammates. Do you support your
teammates? Do you cheer them on and celebrate their successes
and accomplishments? Or do you tend to spread unfortunate news
and pass along the latest gossip? If you have hurt someone through
your gossip, be a big enough person to apologize. Then guard
against making the same mistake in the future by getting your
gossiping under control.

In your dealings with others, remember to praise in public, but
criticize only in private. Any problems should be discussed behind
closed doors and kept among the people you trust most. Leaks of
sensitive information can be extremely destructive. Loose lips do
sink ships. Never forget that you and your teammates are all in the
same boat.

You Gotta Use the Power of Edification

Edification is a key principle for winning. It means to build others
up through your words and actions. The purpose of edification is
to create a protective shield or barrier around the team and the

organization. When people edify each other, they create a bond that cannot be broken, a bond that will be needed to make it through tough times.

Edification is a key reason why some teams and organizations flourish and thrive while others don't. Relationships, sports teams, families, businesses and political parties are built or destroyed by words and actions. If you pay close attention, you'll notice that members of championship teams always edify each other. Team members are constantly giving credit to other players, the coaches, the owners, the sponsors, etc.

The opposite is also true: When people speak poorly of their teammates or the organization, the team breaks down. We see it all too often in sports – a player says something negative about another player or the coach to the media. That usually prompts the "attacked" person to fire back with something negative, and a downward spiral begins.

We all have the power to choose each and every day whether we will build others up or tear them down; whether we will gossip, gripe and complain, or use the power of edification to build a strong and powerful team. It takes careful thought and planning to edify. It takes very little time to destroy. If more people focused on edification, we would have a lot more successful people in the world, and it would be a better place to live.

Edification doesn't mean saying things you don't believe are true or agreeing with everything someone says or does. It's about finding the good qualities that exist in others and then focusing on, and talking about, those positive points. No one is perfect and everyone makes mistakes. Praise and recognize others for the good things they do and be tolerant of the things that make each of us less than perfect.

Unfortunately, looking for the positives doesn't come naturally for most of us. We've become conditioned to look for the negative in every situation. But with some practice, we can all become edification experts. Here are five steps to help you focus on building others up:

1. **Encourage**. Everyone loves to be encouraged. Make a conscious effort to be more positive towards others – lift them up, help them feel more confident and secure, and let them know they are important.

2. **Educate**. If you want people to grow and become better at what they do, consistently give them positive, constructive feedback and provide them with the best tools available to help them win.

3. **Celebrate**. Find ways to recognize achievements with meaningful awards and ceremonies. Create an atmosphere where people want to become successful. This part of edification is fun for everyone and is a great way to build unity and motivate the team.

4. **Console**. Be alert to the problems and needs that surround you. Care about people. Be willing to listen to their problems, hurts and pains, and then build them back up.

5. **Communicate**. Effective communication is the key to the first four steps. Remember: it's not what you say that matters; it's how the message is received. If the person you're communicating with doesn't hear the message you intended to give, you haven't communicated effectively.

If you want to reach the highest level of success, *you gotta* learn to tap into the amazing power of edification. It is the oil that keeps a successful team running smoothly. It creates positive, excited, belief-oriented teams. Learn to give it and receive it well. You will quickly discover that when you edify others, they will begin to edify you in return. Edify others now, and you will see the benefits in the months and years to come.

You Gotta Create Team Synergy

There is amazing power in teams. It's that mysterious, almost magical quality called "synergy." As it relates to teams, synergy means the interaction of two or more people so that their combined output is greater than the sum of their individual efforts and talents. In other words, with synergy $1 + 1 + 1 + 1$ equals a lot more than 4! The magic comes in the "+" sign that joins people together and encourages us to achieve more than we could on our own. Whether you're working with other business people, your spouse and kids, or a group of friends, teamwork creates synergy, and synergy creates excitement and magnification.

Pretend for a moment that you're at the biggest championship game of the year. Your team is at home and winning. As the clock ticks down to the final seconds, thousands of screaming, cheering, excited fans are going nuts. Every part of your body is vibrating, and your endorphins are flowing.

Now imagine being at the same game, at the same moment, but this time there are only four other fans in the entire stadium. When your team wins, what would that experience be like? You may be saying, "It would be great – I'd have the best seats in the house." But the truth is, if there are only five people yelling, "Yeah!" it's not quite the same.

Think about it: How does any event feel when you experience it on your own? I can guarantee it's not nearly as much fun as experiencing it with other people. When you experience things as a team, your team members' excitement adds to your excitement. You could never experience that same level of excitement alone. That's the power of synergy.

Teamwork in business and in life is about sharing – sharing work, ideas, opinions, knowledge, thoughts and feelings. By definition, being on a team means sharing yourself with others and being willing to receive from others. Team synergy comes from the capacity to work with and share with others at a deep level on a continuous basis. Some of these relationships will cause you to grow like you have never grown before. Some will be painful and cause you to look at your life in new and different ways. Some will give you a tremendous sense of contribution. And some will expand your capacity to achieve excellence at a level you never could have accomplished alone.

There is a connection that happens between people when they share. That connection creates the energy that produces results greater than the sum of the individual efforts. When you share as a team, you magnify all that is good. When there is synergy, there is expansion and magnification.

Many human needs can be met through teamwork. Sure, you can achieve some things by yourself, but you will never experience success at the same level of intensity and joy as you will when you achieve victory as a member of a team.

**To win,
you gotta have a team.**

To have a team, *you gotta*:

Be a team player;

Know your role;

Be a little political;

Use the power of edification;

Create team synergy.

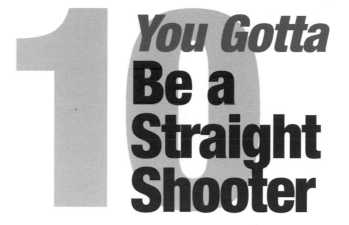

You Gotta Be a Straight Shooter

If you want to win long term, *you gotta* be a "straight shooter." *You gotta* have character and integrity; *you gotta* be honest, forthright, ethical, and trustworthy.

While a quality like honesty is fairly straightforward – either you lie, steal or cheat or you don't – the concept of integrity is not so cut and dried. As with the concept of success, "integrity" means different things to different people because integrity is linked to personal values. As a result, people judge others' integrity based on their own value system.

However, I think there is a certain level of integrity we can all agree on. Integrity is about living up to the standards of your profession, calling, or position. It means being trustworthy, even when no one will ever find out what you've done. It's easy to have integrity when

> *"If you believe in unlimited quality and act in all your business dealings with total integrity, the rest will take care of itself."*
>
> – Frank Perdue

someone is watching. The true test is what you do when no one is around.

Character, on the other hand, goes deeper. Character is about who you are as a person. Character is the ability to follow through with a commitment, goal, or dream long after the excitement of the moment is gone. Integrity influences your behavior, while character is about who you are and where you're going. Being a straight shooter means putting your character into action and living a life of integrity.

You Gotta Maintain Your Integrity

Maintaining your integrity often becomes a critical issue when you succeed because it is then that you may be called upon to compromise your principles. In order to truly win, *you gotta* keep your integrity despite your success.

> *"Integrity is not a 90 percent thing, not a 95 percent thing; either you have it or you don't."*
>
> – Peter Scotese

Developing a reputation for honesty and integrity is something you should strive for simply because it's the right thing to do; but it's also a smart business and sales strategy. People do business with people they like and trust. When you have integrity, your prospects, customers, peers and coworkers will trust you. And the more people trust you, the less risk they feel in working with you.

The truly outstanding salesperson is the one who doesn't misrepresent what the product or service can do. The salesperson with integrity tells prospects when a product or service isn't right for them. Even if a prospect doesn't buy, he or she will always remember the salesperson's integrity. According to Zig Ziglar, "The most important persuasion tool you have in your entire arsenal is integrity."

Don't get me wrong – I've made some mistakes I'm not proud of. What I can tell you is that the agony, dissatisfaction and other negative consequences the low road brought were never worth it. I learned that lesson the hard way. Now I do my best to avoid the low road no matter what instant satisfaction or temporary rewards it may seem to offer. Taking the high road is often not easy or popular, but if you compromise your principles and integrity, it will always end up costing you in the long run.

You Gotta Play by the Rules

Sometimes in the game of life, people become frustrated because they're not achieving their goals fast enough. The success they desire seems so far away. Instead of working harder, they give in to the temptation to cut corners and bend – or even break – the rules. Their desire for success overrides their sense of right and wrong, and they mistakenly think success is worth more than their integrity.

Then there are people who have achieved a certain level of success and think they are above the rules. Many of these individuals followed the rules to get to the top; but once they got there, they felt the rules didn't apply to them anymore. They believe they can continue to ignore the rules and there won't be any consequences, but it's only a matter of time before they get caught.

People who break the rules either to achieve success or because of success have walked away from their integrity. They stop relying on their moral compass to keep them on track. I'm always amazed at superstars who sabotage themselves. Success throws them out of their comfort zone, and they start making bad decisions. In the 1988 Olympics, Canadian sprinter Ben Johnson roared past the competition, broke the world record in the 100 meters and won the gold medal. But when he tested positive for steroids, he was forced to forfeit his medal and his record was erased. His gold was given to silver medalist, American Carl Lewis.

Investigators later discovered that Johnson had been using steroids for several years to improve his performance. He had succumbed to the promise of fame and success that comes with being a world champion. And because he had gotten away with it, he continued to break the rules. The saddest part of the story is that Johnson was eventually banned from the sport. Imagine how different his life could have been if only he had played by the rules.

Just as there are no short cuts to success in sports, there are no short cuts to success in business, in sales or in life. If you're frustrated because you're not achieving your goals fast enough, don't give in to the temptation to break the rules. That's not the answer. You may achieve some short-term success, but your lapse of integrity will come back to haunt you. Instead, go to your coach for advice, change your strategy if necessary, and then work harder.

You Gotta Follow Through

To be a straight shooter, *you gotta* walk the talk. In other words, you have to do what you say you're going to do. You can't say one thing and then do another. There's a big difference between people who are interested and those who are committed. People who are committed will do whatever it takes to follow through.

It's been said that you are only as good as your word. Actually, I think this is only half right. I think it should be, "You are only as good as your word – *if* you do what you say you will do." Your word must be your bond. If you commit to something, follow through. A person who keeps his or her word every time will gain respect from others. But a person who doesn't keep his or her word, even in little things, will earn a negative reputation.

People often think that if they have good intentions they are straight shooters. That's simply not true. You can have all the good intentions in the world, but if you don't act in a way that's consistent with those intentions, your goodwill is meaningless. There's a quote from the book *Walk the Talk* that says: "We judge ourselves mostly by our intentions, but others judge us mostly by our actions. People hear what we say, but they see what we do. And seeing is believing."

Walking the talk is absolutely critical in sales. I've seen a lot of companies with good products that are no longer in business because they didn't follow through on their commitments. To stay in the game, *you gotta* deliver what you promise. In sports if you don't deliver, you'll get cut from the team. In business, you must absolutely deliver on the commitments and obligations you make to customers, even if it means working overtime or losing money. Your ability and willingness to follow through and walk your talk will be key indicators of your success.

> *"You keep customers by delivering on your promises, fulfilling your commitments and continually investing in the quality of your relationships."*
> – Cavett Robert

Some people have a hard time honoring their commitments simply because they haven't learned when and how to say, "No." They make too many promises without thinking about how they're going to fulfill those commitments. This is the type of short-term thinking that gets people in trouble. It is far better to make fewer commitments and keep the ones you do make, than to agree to everything and only be able to deliver on some of it.

Following through is simply the right thing to do, but it also has an unexpected benefit. When you follow through on your commitments (including the commitments you make to yourself), you gain confidence, belief, and momentum.

You Gotta Be Honest with Yourself

Being a straight shooter and following through goes much further than being honest with others. To be a straight shooter you must be completely honest with yourself. You are the most important person to be honest with because self-awareness is the key to improving any area of your business or life.

You are also the *toughest* person to be honest with. Why? Because it's difficult to admit that there are areas of our lives where we're falling short and not living up to the standards we've set for ourselves. To admit there's a problem implies that we should do something about it and that throws us out of our comfort zones. So, we take the path of least resistance and either ignore our problems or rationalize them away. But the rationalizations you tell yourself are exactly the things that keep you from becoming the person you were destined to be. When you rationalize, you try to justify to yourself and others that there are good, valid reasons why you act or behave the way you do.

If you're going to win the game of life, *you gotta* be honest with yourself and admit there are some things that must change. *You gotta* stop rationalizing and get a crystal clear understanding of where you truly are in all areas of your life and business. Self-honesty is the cure for rationalizations. In short, *you gotta* stop sugar coating your lack of achievement and your problems and face them head on!

When you settle for less than who you could be, you settle for a life of mediocrity ... and winners aren't mediocre.

So stop right now and do a gut check. Get rid of the sugar coating and rationalizations and face the hard truth about your hang-ups. See things as they really are. If you're like me, thinking about these things probably makes you uncomfortable ... that's the whole idea. The purpose of this process is to show you the truth, help you break these destructive patterns, and give you the power and the inspiration to change.

> *"As long as a man stands in his own way, everything seems to be in his way."*
> – Ralph Waldo Emerson

On a piece of paper, write down the answers to the following questions.

1. What issues are keeping you from being all that you know deep inside you can be? Consider characteristics, traits, negative habits, poor business practices, relationship problems, etc. What actions or behaviors are inconsistent with the standards and values you've set for yourself personally and professionally? In which areas are you not working hard enough or not committed enough? Which aspects of your life are just not good enough anymore?

2. What rationalizations and reasons do you give yourself for staying in the middle of your mess? How do you sugar coat your problems and hang-ups?

3. What are the reasons why you must stop these rationalizations and break the negative patterns that are holding you back? Is it for your health? Because your family deserves it? Because you know you can do or be so much more? To take your company or team to the next level? To get someone or something back that you've lost? Knowing why you must do something gives you the power and commitment to follow through and make the change.

4. What kind of person do you have to become to move past these issues and achieve the life that most people only dream of? What characteristics, qualities and beliefs must you develop? What actions must you take on a consistent basis? How must you think, talk, act, believe and behave? How must you treat your family, friends, coworkers? How confident must you be?

Now, become that person! Go out and *act as if* you are this "new you." Decide right now to be that person.

In the game of life, your biggest opponent is yourself and your rationalizations. If you will continue to face the truth every day, if you will demand more of yourself than other people expect, if you will keep your integrity and play by the rules, and if you will follow through on your commitments, life will reward you accordingly. Not only will you usually win, but you will do so with a clean conscience. You will have earned self-respect and the respect of others, and you'll feel good about the success you have achieved.

To win,
you gotta be a straight shooter.

To be a straight shooter,
you gotta:

Maintain your integrity;

Play by the rules;

Follow through;

Be honest with yourself.

11 *You Gotta* Stay In to Win

We've all heard the saying,
"Winners never quit and quitters never win." If
you're going to win, *you gotta* get in the game and
you gotta stay in the game. True champions are willing to stick it
out through the ups and the downs, the good and the bad.

Many people believe you've got to be lucky to succeed. This is
exactly the type of mediocre thinking that holds you back and
keeps you from achieving your dreams. Luck is hitting a jackpot
in Las Vegas or winning the lottery. Luck is when something just
falls in your lap. Success is doing the right things long enough
until you finally achieve your goals. If you're betting on luck,
good fortune or it being your "turn" to win, you might hit the
jackpot; then again, you might not. However, if you create your
own luck, your odds of winning increase substantially.

There is only one recipe for creating luck, and it has two ingredients:
hard work and determination. Some people define luck as an
acronym: **L**aboring **U**nder **C**orrect **K**nowledge. But all the
knowledge in the world won't do you any good without hard work
and determination. I would say that luck is laboring, learning from
your mistakes, making slight changes and then pressing on.

To create your own luck, you must be willing to take action, do the work and pay the price of success. Thomas Jefferson said it best: "I find that the harder I work, the more luck I seem to have."

Unfortunately, it's becoming more and more difficult to find people with the determination it takes to become a superstar. We live in a "microwave" society based on fast food and short marriages. Few people are willing to stay in the game when times get tough. Your determination will come from staying focused and being persistent. Getting in the game is important, but staying in the game is the only way to win.

> *"Luck is a matter of preparation meeting opportunity."*
>
> – Unknown

You Gotta Pay the Price

To succeed in athletics, sales, business or anything else, *you gotta* pay the price. To get to the top and stay there takes years of hard work, dedication and commitment. Too many people look at paying the price as a negative, but it should be viewed as a positive. If you will pay the price of success today, you will enjoy the rewards and benefits in the future.

Pick any superstar athlete, and you can bet they paid a price for their success: Years of daily practices. Time in the game, time on the bench. Losing seasons. Blood, sweat and tears – literally. Missing out on fun and family time.

It's just an inescapable fact of life – if you want success, *you gotta* pay the price. Unfortunately, many people think high achievers just wake up one day to instant success. These people have never seen the determined salesperson that makes call after call after call, only to be met with voicemail, rudeness and people who "forgot" he was coming. And yet he does the same thing again the next day. These people have never worked for days to close a sale, only to have it canceled the next morning.

Everyone wants to make the game-winning shot. People want the rewards of owning a successful business. And just about everyone wants to be healthy and physically fit. But, are they willing to put forth the effort to make it happen? Are they willing to do the training and show up every day? Are they willing to work 12 to 16 hours a day, 6 to 7 days a week to get there? Are they willing to pay the price of success?

"There is no substitute for hard work. Genius is one percent inspiration and ninety-nine percent perspiration."
– Thomas Alva Edison

One of my favorite quotes about paying the price is from motivational speaker Les Brown:

> "If you want a thing bad enough to go out and fight for it, to work day and night for it, to give up your time, your peace, and your sleep for it … if all that you dream and scheme is about it, and life seems useless and worthless without it … if you gladly sweat for it and fret for it and plan for it and lose all your terror of the opposition for it … if you simply go after that thing you want with all of your capacity, strength and sagacity, faith, hope and confidence and stern pertinacity … if neither cold, poverty, famine, nor gaunt, sickness nor pain of body and brain, can keep you away from the thing that you want … if dogged and grim you beseech and beset it, with the help of God, you WILL get it!"

There are no shortcuts to success. It always comes with a price. You may love to play golf, go fishing or watch TV, but you can't putt, cast or be a couch potato all day and expect to achieve any true level of success.

You Gotta Stay Focused

If you're going to win the game, *you gotta* stay focused on your dreams and goals. It's a simple idea that's actually very difficult to practice. Why? Because any time you make a decision to do something, you're going to encounter distractions and obstacles. All sorts of resistance can and will show up to steal your time, your attention and eventually your dreams if you let it. The challenge is to ignore the distractions, overcome the obstacles and stay focused on the goal.

Distractions are probably your biggest opponent when it comes to achieving your goals and dreams. And interestingly, it's usually the small day-to-day diversions, those urgent but not important tasks, which are the most distracting. Most people spend too much time doing "second things" first. They get sidetracked, running here and there, confusing busyness with business. They do a thousand things, but they don't accomplish much. And when they do finally get around to working on their goals and dreams, they don't have enough energy or creativity left for the things that affect their lives the most. If your goals and dreams are getting the "leftovers" of your life, you'll never achieve them.

> *"You must remain focused on your journey to greatness."*
>
> – Les Brown

Stay focused by continually asking yourself, "Is what I'm doing moving me toward my goals and purpose? Or am I just spinning my wheels, being busy but not really making any progress?" Use your goals to guide you in prioritizing your time. Otherwise, you'll wander aimlessly through your days, doing whatever urgent tasks come up, instead of completing the steps necessary to move toward your goals.

Let me tell you a story. You may have heard it before, but its message is a good reminder no matter how many times you hear it.

One day, a professor was teaching a class about time management. The professor set a one-gallon glass jar on the table and filled it up with rocks. He asked the class, "Is this jar full?" Of course, the students said, "Yes!" Then he pulled out a bag of pebbles and poured them into the jar. As he did, he shook the jar so that the pebbles sifted down through the holes between the rocks. Eventually, the pebbles reached the top. Again, he asked the class, "Is this jar full?" The students cautiously answered, "Yes."

Next, he pulled out a bag of sand and did the same thing – pouring and shaking, until the sand reached the top of the jar. This time when he asked the class if the jar was full, he got a resounding, "No!" Finally, he pulled out a pitcher of water and poured that into the jar until the water reached the top.

Then he asked the students, "What was the point of this illustration?" One young man jumped up and said, "I know what it is: No matter how full your schedule is, if you try hard enough, you can always fit some more things into it!"

"No," the professor said, shaking his head. "You've missed the point. The truth this illustration teaches us is this: If you don't put the big rocks in first, you'll never get them in at all."

If you fill your jar with pebbles, sand or water first, there will be no room for rocks. The less important things (the "second things") will take up all your time, and you won't ever be able to get the big rocks (your goals and dreams) accomplished. Always schedule those tasks that move you toward your goals *first*. Once your goal-related activities are scheduled, then you can fill in with all those other activities that are less important but still need to be accomplished.

Studies have shown that you should give 80 percent of your time and attention to the top 20 percent of your priorities. That means you should be spending 80 percent of your time on your dreams and goals, and 20 percent of your time on everything else. Do you put your rocks in your jar first, or do you fill your jar with all the little pebbles and sands of distraction?

Another effective strategy for staying focused is to delegate as many "second things" as possible. Most of us tend to think that nobody can do things as well as we can, so we end up doing it all. We spend our energy on things that aren't the best use of our time and talents. Stop getting bogged down with all those things you know you shouldn't be involved with. Focus on your goals and be happy to delegate (and monitor) the rest.

We all have the same precious 24 hours each day. How you choose to use that time is vitally important. Every hour that passes is one less hour you have left to accomplish your goals and dreams. Are you investing your time or wasting it?

You Gotta Keep Your Field of Dreams Green

Throughout my career, I've learned to appreciate and understand the power of focus that high-performance people possess. The movers and shakers don't allow themselves to be distracted by every "good deal" or pie-in-the-sky opportunity that comes along. They understand that if they're going to win, they have to continually focus on their own game.

I get emails, faxes and phone calls every day from people trying to get me interested in different moneymaking deals. I never pursue any of them. People ask me if I feel like I may be missing an opportunity. I tell them I don't know, but I don't have time to worry about it because I'm focused on being the best I can be with the fantastic opportunity I already have.

I have a friend who's always jumping from one opportunity or business to another. To him, the grass is always greener on another field. He's never learned that if you water and fertilize the grass on your own field, it will get greener and you'll want to stay. Sometimes the grass truly is greener somewhere else, but that's only because someone is over there taking care of it!

Take care of the grass on your own field. If you're convinced you've found your "field of dreams," build it! Stop looking for something better and stay focused on the opportunity at hand. If you do, eventually it will become so fresh and desirable that others will want to play on your field.

You Gotta Be Persistent

Most superstars weren't always great, but they were persistent enough to stay in the game and keep improving until they achieved success. Persistence, or perseverance, means continuing in spite of opposition or discouragement.

When you have superstar persistence, you will consistently take action no matter what obstacles or challenges you may face; you will do whatever it takes to achieve your objective and claim victory. Perseverance is one of the key distinctions that separates the superstars from the average in any situation.

Thomas Edison was an unbelievably prolific inventor. He holds more patents (1,093) than any other person in U.S. history. Did you know that Edison and his associates failed more than 9,000 times before finally discovering the secret to the light bulb? It takes amazing persistence to continue to shrug off that kind of failure!

> *"Press on.*
> *Nothing in the*
> *world can take*
> *the place*
> *of persistence."*
>
> *– Ray Kroc*

Colonel Sanders was told "No" more than 1,000 times before he sold his first piece of Kentucky Fried Chicken. At the age of 54, he drove from town to town, restaurant to restaurant, often sleeping in his car, believing his "secret recipe" would eventually pay off. Can you imagine the faith, patience and perseverance it took for him to keep going?

A favorite saying in the sales profession is, "I've got to get my 'No's' out of the way." I know a salesperson who got 21 "No's" in a row. He almost quit. Instead, he was persistent, and his 22nd sales call was successful and launched his career. Three months later, he was National Sales Champion, outselling every other salesperson in his company for that month.

Are you able to keep your mind engaged and persevere through your failures and the "No's"? Will you try to improve with every chance you're given? When you encounter a failure, don't beat yourself up. Do your best to learn from it, make adjustments and continue to take action. Some things have to be learned from experience. Treat each failure as an opportunity to move closer to your goals. If Edison hadn't learned from his 9,000 failures and relentlessly persisted, we might all still be sitting in the dark.

The force behind some of history's boldest achievements is simply this: The diligent will to persevere. Sometimes we refer to this as "sheer determination," or we say someone has "lots of guts." It's all about staying power. It takes great persistence to continue believing in yourself in the face of failure. But don't give up! Keep on trying and you will eventually succeed. Never forget that every "No" is one step closer to a "Yes!"

You gotta stay in to win.

To stay in to win, *you gotta*:

Pay the price;

Stay focused;

Keep your field of dreams green;

Be persistent.

12 You Gotta Overcome Adversity

I've always heard that when life knocks you down you need to land on your back, because if you can look up, you can get up. The defining difference between average performers and superstars is that when superstars get knocked down, they get back up. They refuse to stay down for long. Although bruised and sometimes emotionally wounded, they are able to pick themselves up and start over again.

The world is full of people who claim they could have made it to the big leagues *if only* they had gotten a lucky break or *if only* they hadn't received some kind of injury. They could have made it to the top *if only* the boss wasn't such a jerk, *if only* their parents hadn't brained-washed them, or *if only* their family wasn't so dysfunctional.

> *"Adversity causes some men to break, others to break records."*
> – William Arthur Ward

You can *if only* your life away, or you can decide that you want to live above your circumstances. You can decide that your past will not determine your future.

You Gotta Know There Will Be Challenges

No one wins every game. Every player has slumps and losing streaks. There is not an athlete on the playing field who hasn't overcome problems, injuries and personal trials. Most of us don't realize that most successful people faced challenges and setbacks on their way to success. Every salesperson has bad days, bad weeks and even bad months. Every business has unprofitable quarters. A surprising number of millionaires have been bankrupt at least once in their lives.

We are all going to have times in our lives when we are faced with adversities. Some of them will be small, and we can deal with them immediately. Others will be much bigger – they have the potential to knock us out of the game and send us to the sidelines for healing and comfort. The only difference between temporary setbacks and long-term ones is the amount of down time you decide to give yourself.

> *"Every winner*
> *has scars."*
>
> – Herbert Casson

I have had many adversities in my journey toward success, and I have shared just a few of these with you. But none of them can compare to what happened in the year 2000.

For quite some time, my life had been rolling along smoothly. Our business was successful – I was running a six-state region and our organization was growing at a fast pace. My wife Susan and I had three boys and a brand new baby girl. We had a beautiful house on some land, nice cars, a great church, wonderful friends, etc. Every area of our life seemed to be complete.

Even though my organization was doing well, the company as a whole was facing some challenges. Sales were down for the fifth year in a row and down 50 percent from their all-time highs. The company decided it was time for a change, and I was flattered when I was offered the position of president.

But I was also a little bit nervous. If I accepted the position, we would have to move away from a small city where we had friends, family and support, and relocate to a metropolis with a population of four million where we knew almost no one. It was going to take a lot of dedication, long hours and an entirely new level of commitment on my part to help the company and get sales moving in a positive direction. After many discussions with Susan and a lot of praying, we decided to make the commitment and accept the position.

Just two weeks later came the worst and most trying adversity in my life – the sudden death of our 10-month-old daughter, Skylar. In a tragic set of circumstances, every parent's worst nightmare happened to us, and we lost our precious daughter.

It was something I never could have been prepared for. We were good people   why had this happened to us? Within a few short weeks, our lives went from a dream to a nightmare. I was literally devastated, and I couldn't eat, sleep, drink or think. How was I going to lead my family through this tragedy and at the same time lead our company through its trying times?

You Gotta Learn from Adversity

I'll never understand why Skylar lost her life. What I do know is that there is always something you can learn and some way you can become better because of your adversities. I learned a lot about myself and the power of the human mind and spirit. I learned what was most important in life and that I should never take the good times for granted. I tell my wife and kids I love them a lot more than I used to, and I'm a more caring and compassionate person. My relationships are better than they have ever been before. I've been able to forgive and forget many of the personal issues that I once used as a mental crutch. One example was my relationship with my father. Though our relationship was never bad, there was always room for improvement. But I had never taken the initiative to make it better – I always had the feeling there would be another day, another chance, another opportunity to say the things I wanted to say.

Through the loss of our daughter, I learned you don't always get a second chance. You better make the most of each day and make the most of all the relationships that are important to you. So I decided to spend some time with my father at his favorite meeting place, the lake. While we fished, we talked about life and how everyone makes mistakes. We talked about how we can't change the past, but what we can do is change today, tomorrow, and the rest of our lives. We can learn from our own adversities, and even the adversities of others, and look to the future. And start a new chapter.

Do you have unfinished business, personally or professionally? If you do, I want to encourage you to take whatever steps are necessary to make peace with yourself and others. Life is too short to sit and wait for others to come to you. The power is in the moment – go ahead and make the first move. You'll be glad you did. Remember: the quality of your life is determined by the actions you take.

You Gotta Pick Yourself Up

While you can't always control what happens to you, you can control your response. It's not what happens to you in life, it's how you act or react that makes the difference.

When things go wrong or circumstances are created beyond your control, don't waste valuable time blaming others for what happened. Shift your attention from what is wrong to what the situation could be like in the future. Take a step back and realize that tomorrow is another day. After every down is an up, as surely as the dawn follows the darkness and spring follows winter. Harness the power of words, thoughts and actions to make your optimism and faith in the future more real than your difficulties in the present.

After Skylar's death, I realized I had two choices: I could pick myself up, face my new life and go on; or I could bail out of the president's job and retreat back to what was safe and comfortable. No one would have blamed me if I'd quit; most people didn't even know because my new position hadn't been announced.

I chose to pick myself up and go on. I knew I had to find a purpose where there seemed to be none. I had to find faith when there seemed to be no faith at all. I had to find out what was really important to me and to my family and use that as my motivation. I became more determined than I had ever been in my entire life. I was determined to do it for Skylar, my wife, my children and myself. I had one mission, and that was for my family and me to make it

> *"It is not what happens to you, but how you handle what happens to you that makes the difference."*
>
> – Zig Ziglar

through this tremendously challenging time. It was as though I was being refined in a smelter's furnace.

Most of my friends and family couldn't understand how I could face these challenges so soon after the loss of my daughter. And since then, many people have asked me exactly what I did to overcome such a profound adversity. The truth is, I faced the challenges the same way I had confronted so many other obstacles in my life. I overcame my adversity by:

◆ Making a decision;

◆ Setting some goals;

◆ Taking the first step and then following up with baby steps every day;

◆ Raising the bar and raising my standards;

◆ Working on my attitude every day;

◆ Relying on the caring members of my team;

◆ Focusing on what was right in my life and not what was wrong;

◆ Replacing negative thoughts with positive ones;

◆ Willing myself to stay in the game;

◆ And, most importantly, praying daily – continually asking God for wisdom and strength.

Sound familiar? I know to the depths of my being that the concepts I've shared with you in this book work. I know it because I've applied them during the good times of my life and achieved tremendous results. But I also know you can apply them in your worst times, and they will make you stronger and see you through to a new season.

When you experience adversity (and at some point, everyone will experience adversity), *you gotta* step back and take time to heal. It's okay to have some "down time," but don't let yourself get in a rut or slump you can't pull out of. Be sure to set a date to get back in the game. You must pick yourself up, face your fears head on, examine your priorities, set new objectives and goals, get refocused and maybe even mend some fences. These simple steps will help you be productive again and get your momentum back.

During the down times, it's crucial that you read inspirational books about overcomers, people who have achieved great things in spite of great challenges and adversities. Listen to motivational audios and seek counsel from your coach or mentor. As you conquer each challenging day, you will be able to see daylight again. Eventually you will emerge a stronger, more powerful and more compassionate person.

You Gotta Make A Comeback

Skylar's death taught me that no matter how bad the pain is, if you're willing to make an effort – and at times it may require a fierce effort – you can come back bigger, better and stronger. Lance Armstrong did.

In 1996, although he had never won the Tour de France (the most prestigious race in cycling), Lance Armstrong was the number one ranked cyclist in the world. But in October of that year, Lance discovered he had advanced testicular cancer that had spread to his lungs and brain. Chances for his recovery were less than 50 percent. He endured two surgeries, including brain surgery, and chemotherapy. Although he was weak, Lance started to think about racing again only five months after his diagnosis. Unfortunately, to add insult to injury, his sponsor had dropped him.

But Lance didn't let that stop him. He decided to make a comeback. In 1998, he declared victory over cancer and returned to racing. The road back was long and hard, with many challenges and discouragements. But just one year later, in 1999, Lance won the Tour de France. Amazingly, he is now the only person in history to have won the race seven years in a row. What a comeback!

The question is, if Lance Armstrong had never experienced the adversity of cancer, would he have become the greatest cyclist in history? In his book *Every Second Counts,* he gives us the answer: "I've often said that cancer was the best thing that ever happened to me ... the fact is that I wouldn't have won even a single Tour de France without the lesson of illness."

Depending on how you choose to react to adversity, it can make you stronger and better, and you can make a comeback.

Approximately one year after Skylar's death, Susan and I wanted to make our own comeback. We decided to try and have another child. However, Susan's tubes had been tied and couldn't be reversed. So, after careful consideration and consultation, we decided to try in vitro fertilization. But after numerous attempts, Susan still wasn't pregnant. Miraculously, the very last embryo remaining implanted and Susan became pregnant.

There were many complications during her pregnancy, including a near miscarriage, and Susan was in and out of the hospital for six months. Then, when she was seven months pregnant, she had serious complications and had to be flown by helicopter to the hospital. But two weeks later – only one year, 11 months, and 17 days after Skylar's death – our family was truly blessed with the birth of our daughter, Destany.

Because she was premature, Destany had to stay in the hospital for almost a month. But the day she finally came home healthy and happy was one of the greatest moments in our lives. After everything our family had been through, to be able to have, hold, feel and see this precious miracle was a true testament to the power of faith, hope, belief and perseverance.

At the same time, our company was making its own comeback. Only seven months after Destany was born, the company had the best year in its 32-year history, and we broke almost every sales record. The following year, we broke our sales record again. In sports they call that "back-to-back wins." The next year, we did it again – we had our third consecutive record-breaking year. I guess you could say we had a "three-peat."

I wanted to share the story of my biggest adversity and how my family and I made personal, professional and psychological comebacks, to let you know that after the rain and the pain there will be brighter days. If you are experiencing adversities in your life, look deep inside for strength and continue the journey. Always keep your faith. Accept your adversities and understand that they are preparing you for your ultimate purpose. Remember that God's delays aren't necessarily God's denials.

"Things don't go wrong and break your heart so you can become bitter and give up. They happen to break you down and build you up so you can be all that you were intended to be."

– Charlie "Tremendous" Jones

Adversity doesn't have to be the beginning of the end. *You gotta get past the starting line* – or even the "re-starting line" – if you're ever going to reach the finish line. It's no disgrace to start again. It can even be an opportunity to step back, evaluate your situation and then reshape your dreams and goals.

Don't allow adversity to **steal** your dream – don't even let it **conceal** your ultimate purpose. Instead, use adversity to **reveal** to you the inner resources you didn't even know you possessed. Use adversity to **peel** back your dream to its foundations – to inspect it for its flaws – and to rededicate yourself to making that dream **real**.

Adversity is a testing of your mettle, your spirit, your character and your courage. Through the flames of shock, disappointment and even loss, you will emerge either "refined" or "resigned." You will have turning points – forks in the road when the decisions you make will determine your ultimate destiny. Adversity can clarify your vision and reignite your purpose and passion. Or, it can give you the excuse you need to retire to the sidelines and seek the sympathies of all the others who are sitting on the bench. Always remember that despite seemingly insurmountable odds, you can overcome your adversities, make a comeback, and win the game.

To win,
you gotta overcome adversity.

To overcome adversity,
you gotta:

Know there wiil be chaiienges;

Learn from adversity;

Pick yourself up;

Make a comeback.

Why Not You?

Success to me means living life with purpose, passion and power. It also means constantly improving the quality of your life and building meaningful relationships with family, friends and business associates. Success means having freedom – the freedom to do what you want, when you want and how you want.

Pursuing your goals and dreams is what the game of life is all about. But you need to keep in mind that no one, not even the most amazing superstar, wins every single game. And rarely does a team have a perfect season. **So just because you may lose a game here and there doesn't mean you're not a winner.**

Winning is really about the lessons you learn and the personal growth you achieve as you play the game. It's about developing as a person, stretching your abilities and becoming a better you. It means that when the game is over, you will be a dramatically different person from who you were when the game began.

> *"If you can dream it, you can do it. Never lose sight of the fact that this whole thing was started by a mouse."*
> – Walt Disney

The truth is, if you're not growing, you're moving backwards, especially in today's ever-changing world. There is no status quo. The key is to constantly strive for improvement. If you start to slip back, take action quickly to stop the slide, analyze the situation and set a new course. Even if you have to take teeny-tiny steps at first, the smallest progress is far better than any movement backwards.

As you pursue your goals and dreams, there is a good chance you will create a ripple effect in your life. In other words, your growth and development will have unintentional effects on those around you. Some of these effects may seem negative at first, like growing apart from friends and family who refuse to grow along with you. But most of the changes will be positive and welcomed. As you grow and stretch, you bring others along with you. You will find that your spouse, your children, and your family and friends will grow along with your success. It truly is a win/win outcome.

If you're going to fulfill your destiny, *you gotta* get in the game, *you gotta* stay in the game and *you gotta* follow the game plan. You already have all the talent and ability you need to win. But *you gotta* take action if you want to realize your goal of winning. Throughout this book, I've laid out a step-by-step plan that will virtually guarantee your success – *if* you will put it into action.

The best thing about winning is coming to the realization that the game is not over. Instead, winning just means you can step back for a moment, enjoy the season, regenerate yourself, and start a new game with new goals and a different set of challenges. Success merely changes the game.

You Can Do It!

Today is the first day of the rest of your life. It doesn't matter what happened yesterday or the day before or five minutes ago. You can't change the past. What you can do is change now, change tomorrow, change the next day, the next month and the rest of your life.

In the future, there will be new superstars in your particular game. Some of them may even go on to nationwide fame. These superstars will be the individuals who consistently take action and follow through with what they learn. Will you be one of them?

"You were born to win; but to be the winner you were born to be, you must plan to win and prepare to win. Then, and only then, can you legitimately expect to win."

– Zig Ziglar

Don't be a spectator in the game of life. You can be a champion, a real superstar. You can live the life you've always dreamed of. It's truly your choice. It all comes down to a decision, a clear unequivocal decision. *You gotta* decide today to do whatever it takes to get off the bench and ***Get in the Game!***

About the Author

For nearly two decades, Billy Cox has dedicated his life to helping others achieve their dreams. He is a leading authority on sales excellence and an expert in helping individuals and organizations achieve peak performance. Billy started in sales and marketing when he was just 17 years old. Over a period of 15 years, he worked his way to the top of every sales and management level, eventually becoming president of the same company. When he took over as President, sales were down 50 percent from their all-time highs. Working as a team, Billy and the other company leaders used the powerful concepts and techniques presented in this book to achieve record sales in only two and a half years.

Billy is a "no limits" person who knows how to win, and he can teach you how to do the same. His hands-on experience and proven track record make him one of the best success coaches in America today. He is a master salesman, a compelling motivator and an energetic leader who believes that if you're going to win, *you gotta get in the game*!

Billy considers his personal accomplishments to be just as important as his professional achievements. He regularly donates his time and talents to youth sports, community service work and various charities. He believes that being involved in sports activities is important for children because it teaches them attitudes and skills that will benefit them for the rest of their lives. Together with his wife, Susan, and their four children, Billy lives in the suburbs of Dallas, Texas.

Six ways to bring the *Get in the Game* message to your team

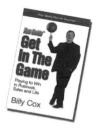

1. Keynote Presentations
Let author Billy Cox personally inspire and empower your organization, team or conference attendees with the powerful message of *Get in the Game*. A keynote with Billy is truly a learning experience that is motivational, interactive, fun, and specifically targeted to generate excitement, shift attitudes, and maximize performance.

2. Workshops
Facilitated by a certified instructor, this three- or six-hour foundation-building program will show every team member, new or experienced, how to apply the ***Get in the Game*** concepts and strategies. These workshops are highly interactive and customized to your team's environment and challenges.

3. *Get in the Game* PowerPoint® Presentation $99.95
You can introduce and reinforce the ***Get in the Game*** concept with your organization with this easy-to-use, cost-effective presentation tool. All the key concepts and ideas from the book are highlighted in this professionally produced, **downloadable PowerPoint presentation that includes a facilitator guide and notes**. Use the presentation for kick-off meetings, training sessions, or as a follow-up developmental tool.

4. *You Gotta Get in the Game* Audio CD Set $19.95
Many people won't take the time to read an entire book, but they will listen to an audio. This unabridged version of the book includes bonus material from author Billy Cox not included in the book.

5. *Playing In the Majors* Audio CD $9.95
This audio will teach your team how to stay focused on high-impact activities and how to quit majoring in the minor tasks that don't contribute to long-term success.

6. Free *Get in the Game* Tools
Log on to **www.YouGottaGetInTheGame.com** for free tools to help you get in the game, stay in the game and win!

For more information on keynotes and workshops or to order products, contact us at:

www.YouGottaGetInTheGame.com
1.800.722.4685
1.972.899.2458
Email: info@YouGottaGetInTheGame.com

Get on the fast track to living your dreams with

The Dream Book
$14.95

"One of the goals in my Dream Book *was to be among the Top 10 Salespeople. When I achieved that goal, I increased it to be among the Top 5. When I reached that, I raised it to be the #1 salesperson ... and I achieved #1!"*
D. S. – Texas

When Billy Cox created *The Dream Book* over 10 years ago, little did he know he had discovered one of the most complete and advanced technologies for personal and professional achievement. Billy's power-packed goal setting technology gives you the ability to change any area of your life and allows you to generate consistent and predictable results. If you've ever dreamed of living a life without limits, *The Dream Book* will show you how you can be, do, have, achieve and create anything you want for your life.

The Dream Book has been credited with helping thousands of people change their lives for the better. It will engage your senses and show you how to effectively use your dreams and goals to achieve the success you desire in six key areas: Health and Fitness, Lifestyle, Career, Finances, Relationships, Mental and Spiritual. No matter what your dreams and goals, you can achieve them if you will commit to following the concepts and principles in ***The Dream Book***. Follow the simple steps outlined in this book, and you will:

- Understand and apply the psychology of goal setting;
- Achieve faster results with more precision;
- Capture the magic moments on your journey to success;
- Experience the joy and fulfillment that comes from living your dreams.

Making the Dream Book Work Audio CD Set

Let Billy Cox personally coach you through the dream-building process with this powerful companion product for *The Dream Book*. **$19.95**

"Buy a house and land ... achieved. Send the children to private school ... achieved. Spend quality time with my wife and kids ... achieved. The Dream Book *has helped us create many memories that most people won't ever get the chance to experience."* D. K. – Missouri

"I had a goal to quit smoking. DONE!" J. J. – Washington

"I set goals to be the number one salesperson in the world and to break our company's 30-year sales record. I wrote these goals down in my Dream Book, *and the next year I accomplished both of them!"* Y.H. – Utah

Order your ***Dream Book*** and **CD** on the order form at the back of this book, call 1.888.789.LEAD (5323) or visit us at www.**CornerStoneLeadership**.com.

Other CornerStone Sales & Customer Service Resources:

Monday Morning Customer Service takes you on a journey of eight lessons that demonstrate how to take care of customers so they keep coming back. **$14.95**

180 Ways to Walk the Customer Service Talk is one resource that you will want to read and distribute to every person in your organization. It is packed with powerful strategies and tips to cultivate world-class customer service. **$9.95**

Goal Setting for Results addresses the fundamentals of setting and achieving your goals. **$9.95**

Customer at the Crossroads offers an entertaining way to reinforce key customer service values. It concludes with a series of thought-provoking questions, making it an effective vehicle for team discussions or reading groups. **$9.95**

Influential Selling – How to Win in Today's Selling Environment will change your sales perspective forever. It is designed to stimulate new ways of thinking about your selling efforts and positioning them to align with your client. It will provide your team with new strategies and activities that will help you start winning today. **$14.95**

136 Effective Presentation Tips provides you with inside tips from two of the best presenters in the world on how to accomplish your objective during every presentation. **$9.95**

Orchestrating Attitude translates the incomprehensible into the actionable. It cuts through the clutter to deliver inspiration and application so you can orchestrate your attitude … and your success. **$9.95**

The CornerStone Perpetual Calendar, a compelling collection of quotes about leadership and life, is perfect for office desks, school and home countertops. **$12.95**

The CornerStone Leadership Collection of Cards is designed to make it easy for you to show appreciation for your team, clients and friends. The awesome photography and your personal message written inside will create a lasting impact. Pack of 30 (6 styles/5 each) **$34.95** *Posters also available.*

Visit www.**CornerStoneLeadership**.com
for additional books and resources.

☑ YES! Please send me extra copies of *You Gotta Get In The Game*!
1-30 copies $14.95   31-100 copies $13.95   100+ copies $12.95

You Gotta Get In The Game	____ copies X_____	= $ _____
You Gotta Get In The Game Audio CD set	____ sets X $19.95	= $ _____
The Dream Book	____ copies X $14.95	= $ _____
Making The Dream Book Work Audio CD set	____ sets X $19.95	= $ _____
Playing In The Majors Audio CD	____ copies X $ 9.95	= $ _____

Additional Sales & Customer Service Resources

Sales & Customer Service Package   ____ packs X $129.95   = $ _____
   (includes *Get In The Game* and one each
   of the items listed on the previous page)

Other Books

_____	____ copies X _____	= $ _____
_____	____ copies X _____	= $ _____
_____	____ copies X _____	= $ _____
	Shipping & Handling	$ _____
	Subtotal	$ _____
	Sales Tax (8.25%-TX Only)	$ _____
	Total (U.S. Dollars Only)	$ _____

Shipping and Handling Charges

Total $ Amount	Up to $49	$50-$99	$100-$249	$250-$1199	$1200-$2999	$3000+
Charge	$6	$9	$16	$30	$80	$125

Name _____ Job Title _____

Organization _____ Phone _____

Shipping Address _____ Fax _____

Billing Address _____ Email _____

City _____ State _____ ZIP _____

❑ Please Invoice (Orders over $200) Purchase Order Number (if applicable)_____

Charge Your Order: ❑ MasterCard   ❑ Visa   ❑ American Express

Credit Card Number _____ Exp. Date _____

Signature _____

❑ Check Enclosed (Payable to: CornerStone Leadership)

Fax	**Mail**	**Phone**
972.274.2884	P.O. Box 764087	888.789.5323
	Dallas, TX 75376	

www.**CornerStoneLeadership**.com

CornerStone
Leadership Institute